FACIN E
BRYANT

PLAYERS, COACHES, AND BROADCASTERS RECALL THE GREATEST BASKETBALL PLAYER OF HIS GENERATION

EDITED BY SEAN DEVENEY

Foreword by Jerry West

SPORTS
PUBLISHING

Sports Publishing books may be purchased in bulk at special discounts for sales promotion, corporate gifts, fund-raising, or educational purposes. Special editions can also be created to specifications. For details, contact the Special Sales Department, Sports Publishing, 307 West 36th Street, 11th Floor, New York, NY 10018 or sportspubbooks@skyhorsepublishing.com.

Sports Publishing® is a registered trademark of Skyhorse Publishing, Inc.®, a Delaware corporation.

Visit our website at www.sportspubbooks.com.

10 9 8 7 6 5 4 3 2 1

Library of Congress Cataloging-in-Publication Data is available on file.

Cover design by Tom Lau
Cover photo credit Associated Press

ISBN: 978-1-61321-977-5
Ebook ISBN: 978-1-61321-980-5

Printed in the United States of America

CONTENTS

FOREWORD

Jerry West

IT HAS BEEN talked about plenty of times, the initial impressions I had of Kobe Bryant. We brought him in for a workout (ahead of the draft in 1996), and you could see after a few minutes that he was head and shoulders above everybody else we had been looking at. I do not want to make it sound like I saw something special or that I saw something other people couldn't see. It was not something I saw. It was something inside of him. Some people have it, some people don't. Kobe was so talented, even at a young age, and it was pretty evident when you watched him as a seventeen-year-old kid, he was extraordinarily gifted as an athlete. Anyone could have seen that. But he was more gifted as a young skilled player. A lot of young players are terrific athletes but they don't have the skill level he did. Honestly, a lot of *veteran* players don't have the skill level he did. But he combined two elements, regardless of the skill level you have, regardless of the physical gifts that you have: one, his work ethic was second to none, and two, his competitive desire was second to none. That really separates the men from the boys.

He was the most talented player I had seen in a long time. You can have great skill, but if you do not have the work ethic you are not going to accomplish anything in your life. I do not care what you're doing. He was an exceptionally gifted young man. When he was born, he was a prodigy kid, and he just needed to find his own niche. His niche happened to be basketball, and he found it. But the work ethic he has shown was exceptional. You can have great skill, but if you don't have work ethic, you are just going to tease everybody about what your potential is. Anyone who is great at anything has a work ethic—and really, there are a lot of players who have a great work ethic but did not have the skill Kobe Bryant had. The combination of those two made him what he was.

I knew his father, Joe, a little bit even before we drafted Kobe, though I did not know him well. I still run into Joe once in a while, and he still likes to play basketball; that gives you an idea of what the game meant to him. He had a passion, too, but he did not have the "it" factor that his son had. But then, few have that. That's just the genetic makeup, where somewhere along the way, someone is gifted in a unique way, someone winds up with all the attributes that make him or her just right, and Kobe had that. Everything was lined up with him. But one of the things you could see was that the parents were very open to encouraging their kids to explore their own talents but also to be exposed to the rest of the world and not be limited. I think Kobe was affected by growing up in Italy (where his father played for seven seasons), not growing up in this country, seeing the world from a different perspective at a very young age, understanding other countries and being able to speak to people in another language. It makes you more worldly, it makes you more experienced, it gives you a different outlook. Any kind of different background, any kind of different experience will let you grow in a way that other experiences can't match.

That was always evident in Kobe, as a person, even if people did not always see that all the time. If you listen to him talk, or interact with the press, he is always very glib, very sharp. He is very bright. He can go into a situation and grasp it right away. He understands people. But he is very well-rounded when it comes to a number of different subjects. Maybe he did not publicly engage that way, but at the same time, what happens—unfortunately—is that a lot of people will pigeon-hole athletes and treat them as though the only thing they can talk about with some knowledge is their sport. Or they can only ask about the things they've accomplished on the court and how they've gone about accomplishing those things. But Kobe is a good example of a player who has a real natural curiosity and intelligence. He will talk with anyone about the things that interest him beyond basketball. He is very well rounded that way.

It was rewarding to watch him as a player over the course of his career. But it was rewarding to get to know him as a person, too. The résumé he built in the league, it is impressive, and it is made even more impressive when you understand that he worked so hard to achieve those things. It took a lot of desire to do the things he did. But it was satisfying to watch him grow. He went from a precocious teenager to an incredibly accomplished pro. In his career, he was remarkable, because you never think somebody is going to play for twenty years, and in particular with the passion and tremendous amount of hard work he put into it, in addition to all the playoff series, the championships he won. You just don't think that someone can do that for twenty years. But he did, and now he is someone who has inspired millions of people and has become one of the iconic players in the history of basketball.

INTRODUCTION

THERE WERE 46 seconds left in Game 7 of the 2000 Western Conference finals when Kobe Bryant lined up Scottie Pippen of the Blazers just inside of half-court at the Staples Center. The series had been an adventure for the Lakers, who got off to a 3–1 lead and were in control of the series, but began losing their grip with a loss on their home floor in Game 5 and a wire-to-wire defeat in Game 6. Coughing up this series would have spelled disaster in Los Angeles, where the Lakers had won 67 games under new coach Phil Jackson and were determined to shed their image as a flashy team that could win in the regular season but folded in the big moments. They'd fought back from a 13-point deficit to open the fourth quarter, and after Pippen missed a three-pointer, they were holding a four-point lead, looking for the knockout blow. That was when Bryant dribbled to the right, getting Pippen to follow him, and crossed back to the left, leaving Pippen well behind him. As Bryant drove inside the three-point line, Portland's Brian Grant stepped into the lane to help. That left Lakers center Shaquille O'Neal open on the right side. O'Neal briefly raised his right hand and made eye contact with Bryant, who drove into the paint. Bryant flipped the ball high over Grant, and O'Neal, leaping and as fully outstretched as a 340-pound man can be, got his hand on the ball and dunked it through. The Lakers went up by six. The knockout punch had been delivered.

After the game, Bryant confessed that he thought he'd blown the play. "I thought I threw the ball too high," he said. "Shaq went up and got it, I was like, 'Damn!'"

As much as any moment in Bryant's 20-year history in the NBA, the alley-oop to O'Neal might have been the most important and the most telling. It was Bryant at his finest, a highlight play in what was his breakout season, the year in which he became more than just O'Neal's sidekick, but a star in his own right, on par with O'Neal. He averaged 22.5 points that year, with 6.3 rebounds and 4.9 assists, coming through with a defining performance when the Lakers most needed him, delivering 25 points, 11 rebounds, seven assists, and four blocked shots in the series finale to get the Lakers a win the franchise desperately needed. Bryant didn't just collect gaudy numbers in that game—he grew up. He had taken his star turn and would only build his legend from there. Of course, he also elbowed his way to the top of the Lakers' hierarchy, establishing an awkward footing alongside O'Neal, a balance that could not be sustained long term. But at that moment future turmoil was far off, and after the game O'Neal said of Bryant, "Kobe's a great player." As he considered the thrill of playing for an NBA championship, Bryant delivered a jolting reminder of just how young he was, just how many thrilling moments were still in his future. "It's something I've dreamed about all of my 21 years," he said. He was 37 when he retired.

The legacy of Kobe Bryant is embedded in moments like these, a litany of them that built his sterling career. Bryant scored 33,643 points, each with its own story. There were the buzzer-beaters he knocked down without blinking, the free throws that gave him points No. 80 and 81 in his career-high game, the shots he had to make after he tore his Achilles tendon, the points he gathered in winning his two scoring championships. Every assist, every rebound, every steal, every block, and even every turnover—they were all part of building the story of Bryant's greatness. And they all came with a price. The stories of Bryant's offseason work ethic are legendary, and his desire to hone his game no matter where he was, no matter the time of night, fueled his greatness. The numbers he collected are a key part of his legacy, but behind those numbers are countless hours spent sweating in the gym, countless shots hoisted to perfect his stroke, countless reps in the weight room. Pure talent is certainly part of Bryant's legacy, but more important was the work put in to get the most out of that talent.

The stories and opinions in this book attempt to offer different viewpoints on Bryant over the course of his career, ways to illuminate the different parts of Bryant's time in basketball.

It begins with his high school coach telling tales of Bryant's early dedication to the game, how he would come to school to work out even on snowy days, how he would make certain he won every wind sprint in practice, how much losing stung him. It traverses his entire career: the success he had with the Lakers when teamed up with Shaquille O'Neal and the eventual breakup of that team; through the 2005-06 season and his 81-point game; the Lakers' return to greatness after acquiring Pau Gasol and reaching three consecutive NBA Finals; the pain of losing one of those Finals to the Celtics; and his thrilling 60-point career finale to close the 2016 season. It includes the memories of role players and Hall of Famers, those who knew Bryant well and those who observed him from afar. It's a safe bet that, if you talk with anyone in the game in the late-1990s and 2000s, they will have a story or strong opinion involving Bryant.

But maybe the most important part of the book comes at the close. That section features players and executives talking about Bryant and the impact he has had pushing the game of basketball onto the global stage, and how he has influenced a future generation of players both with his style of play and with his words of advice and encouragement. The moments and memories from Bryant's 20 years on the court are numerous, and his career will be immortalized. But even after his retirement, Bryant's impact carries on in the betterment of the NBA and its players. As much as any story, statistic, or memory, that will be Bryant's legacy.

PART 1:

KOBE RISES

"**K**OBE WAS ALWAYS trying these unbelievable attempts in practices, and Del (Harris) would get mad and tell him to take the easy shot and make the easy play. But he was a rookie who was not playing. He wanted to make the spectacular play. He was trying to prove himself to Del, like, 'I can do this, but you are still not going to play me?'" –*Cedric Ceballos*

Truth and fiction get muddled with the passage of time, and memory can sometimes leave honest folks with truths that have been twisted, rendered into what we might *like* to have happened rather than what did happen. We know this: the Charlotte Hornets chose Kobe Bryant with the No. 13 pick in the 1996 draft and subsequently traded him to the Lakers for big man Vlade Divac. That was how Bryant's entry into the NBA came about. We know, too, that after Charlotte made the pick, and in the space between the draft choice and the execution of the trade, there was a telephone conversation between Bryant and new Hornets coach Dave Cowens.

During Bryant's final season, in December 2015, Bryant recalled an unpleasant brusqueness to the Cowens call. It seemed Cowens wanted no piece of Bryant, and Bryant remembered Cowens telling him, "We don't really need you here." Bryant added that he used the snub from the Hornets to fuel himself during his early years, turning on his "killer instinct." It's a convenient and easy-to-follow story, one that helps explain the immense drive and determination Bryant showed throughout his NBA career, right from the beginning.

But Cowens's problem with Bryant's recollection is that he says it's simply not true. Cowens recalled a short conversation in which he and Bryant acknowledged the impending trade between the Hornets and Lakers. He would never, Cowens insists, call a newly drafted rookie and talk down to him, nor would he insult him by telling him he's not needed. He did not do so with Bryant. "Why would I do that?" Cowens wondered. "I was a player once. I try to treat all players with some respect."

Ah, the haze of memory. Peeling back the source of Bryant's so-called killer instinct, it's likely that Bryant set up a straw man—that he was looking for motivation and took his draft night "snub" in that light. In fact, the run-up to the 1996 draft was marked by the steering of Bryant toward the Lakers' waiting arms, pulled off by Bryant's agent. In retrospect, the Divac-Bryant swap was a pretty terrible deal from Charlotte's perspective, but Cowens said the Hornets, or any other team in the league for that matter, would have had little choice. Everyone knew that Bryant's agent was telling teams that Bryant would play for no one else but the Lakers or Sixers, an assertion backed up by another front-office executive at the time, Stu Jackson, formerly of the Vancouver Grizzlies. Bryant had done the pre-draft workout circuit and impressed teams mightily along the way, but there was not much chance he'd play for those teams.

That is why Bryant fell out of the Top 10 in the 1996 draft in the first place. No one wanted to take the chance that he would hold out until traded to the Lakers. Bryant's camp had issued a threat to undesirable teams seeking to choose Bryant against his wishes, stating that he'd gladly go play in Italy if the wrong team picked him, a frequently used bit of leverage in pre-draft machinations at the time. It was not an empty threat in the case of Bryant, who had grown up in Italy and was fluent in Italian.

As Cowens still points out to those asking about the trade, "We picked 13th. Everyone asks why we picked Kobe and traded him, but no one ever asks the other 12 teams what happened with them, why they skipped him. Because he wasn't going to play for those other teams."

In the end, Bryant got his wish: he landed with the Lakers, who had become enamored of his talent. Well-regarded Hall of Fame player and team president Jerry West had seen Bryant in a pre-draft workout for just a few minutes before deciding that Bryant was good enough to play in the NBA immediately, even at age 17. That started the Lakers' journey toward making Bryant their franchise centerpiece, showing daring foresight in allowing the fate of the team to rest in the hands of a talented, but utterly untested, teenager. Of course, the Lakers also reeled in a big free-agent catch that summer, bringing in the most dominant big man in the league, Shaquille O'Neal, from the Magic and laying the groundwork for the kind of powerful inside-out combination that would evoke memories of West himself teaming up with Wilt Chamberlain.

Skipping college and going right from high school to the NBA was still fairly new in 1996, with Kevin Garnett having done it the previous year playing for the Timberwolves. But Bryant would have an all-too-common problem in L.A., trying to get playing time on a team that had veterans ahead of him and a coach, Del Harris, who mostly refused to play rookies, let alone teenaged ones. Still, Bryant kept his cool, kept his professionalism intact to a remarkable degree given his circumstances, and mostly kept to himself. In fact, Bryant was so private in his early NBA years that teammates would wonder to other guys around the league why their new young rookie had no interest in the common camaraderie of his teammates, or the rituals— dinner, movies, trips to the mall—that stoked that camaraderie.

But the big issue for the Lakers, for Bryant's first two seasons, remained when the team would finally play Bryant. He often seemed anguished without game action, to both teammates and opponents alike, and West had to nudge Harris more than once to give Bryant some action. When Bryant did get a chance to take the floor, in practice or during short stretches in actual games, there was sometimes calamity and sometimes brilliance. The brilliance was there late in his rookie season, when he scored 24 points in 25 minutes, making nine of his 11 shots, in a blowout over the Warriors. But the calamity was there, too, as in the 1997 playoffs against the Jazz, in which Bryant hurled four air balls, including three in the final minute of overtime, in a Game 5 loss in the conference semifinals.

There were other times, though, where he was able to show flashes of what he could do with a basketball. And it could be thrilling. "You could tell from the beginning," former guard Blue Edwards said, "he had a live body. He had a lot of basketball in him, it just needed to get out."

Gregg Downer
Coach

Résumé: *Downer has been the head basketball coach at Lower Merion High School since 1990, and in his time at the school his teams have won three state championships, including two in*

2013 and 2006, also finishing as runners-up in 2012 and 2005. Downer has helped dozens of players to college basketball scholarships, including one, Darryl Reynolds, who helped Villanova win a national championship this season. But it is the great player from Lower Merion who opted not to go to college, Kobe Bryant, who defined Downer's early tenure as the school's coach, and whose connection to Lower Merion has helped sustain the program since.

Kobe connection: Downer first came across Bryant when he was in middle school, but even long after Kobe left Lower Merion, his connection with Downer remained strong. Bryant donated more than $400,000 to the school to build a basketball court, and in December 2010, Lower Merion christened its new Kobe Bryant Gym. As his NBA career wound up, Bryant frequently reflected back on his high school days, telling USA Today, "Lower Merion and everything associated with it made me who I am." In the next-to-last game of his career, played at Oklahoma City, the Thunder had Downer narrate a tribute video to Kobe. Downer called Bryant "a man who goes by many names, a man described in many ways. But there's only one word that matters most, and that is legacy." The Bryant legacy began with Downer and the Lower Merion Aces.

I MET HIM WHEN he was 13 years old, he was an eighth grader. He was playing out at our junior high school. There was a fair amount of buzz about a good player down there. So I went and thought I would have a look. I watched him play, and of course I was impressed, so I invited him to practice with my varsity players. Five minutes into that workout, he was so good I turned to my assistant coaches and I said, "This kid is a pro." He was 13. I was very impressed very quickly, and I knew right away I had something very special on my hands. His 6-foot-10 father, Joe, was standing in the corner, so I had a hunch what Kobe was, genetically. He was so fundamentally good at the age of 13, and I thought to myself that he was going to get nothing but taller and stronger, and I could tell I had something special and unique.

I had been a fan of Joe Bryant and all the Sixers when I was growing up. I was a 12-year-old season-ticket holder. I would sit in Section H and cheer for Joe Bryant and my 76ers. I was a big NBA fan, a big Sixers fan, I was fortunate to grow up in a good time for Philadelphia basketball. The funny thing is, little did I know at that time, at the end of the row my family and I used to sit in, that was where Kobe's grandfather would sit, Joe Bryant's dad. He had tickets right near ours. On that Sixers team, there was Dr. J, George McInnis, Doug Collins, World B. Free—and I was just a little wide-eyed kid who loved basketball. I definitely knew who Joe was from his playing career, then I got to know him as Kobe's father, too, later on down the road at Lower Merion.

When I got to know Kobe, as good as he was just naturally and physically, what was special was the work ethic. How seriously he took everything even at a young age. He knew what he wanted, he wanted to be a basketball player and he was going to give himself every chance to do that. I saw his hatred of losing, too, and you don't usually see that in a kid so young. I am going on my 27th year at Lower Merion High School, and I have never seen anything, really, similar to his work ethic. I have never seen really anything similar to his hatred of losing. I am similar in that I am ultracompetitive and I hate to lose. From a coaching perspective, I like to think I have a pretty good work ethic, also. When the two of us started to get to know each other, I think that kind of bonded us. It was always nice to know with that team that there were always at least two of us who hated to lose.

I try to push the best player on the team the same I would push the worst player on the team. If you are in a situation where your best player is your hardest-working player—in this case, Kobe—by far, a guy who is winning all the sprints, in the weight room, showing up to school at 6 a.m.—when your best player is the hardest worker, it makes it easier on the coach. He sets the standard, so you don't have to. We would have late school openers for snow, for example, and he would come to school anyway and be in the weight room, he would come in the snow. First to practice, last to leave practice, winning every drill and sprint. He was lifting weights, even as a young guy, at a time when lifting weights really wasn't done for basketball players. And it wasn't the Lakers' practice facility. It was a dingy old basement, there wasn't a lot of heat down there and the equipment was not that good, that was our weight room in our old gym. But he was down there. A lot of kids, you have to kind of force into the weight room, but that was never the case with him. If he felt there was something he could do to make himself better at this sport, he was going to do it.

He didn't joke around much, he didn't waste a lot of time. He has a nice, big personality, and he can be jovial when he wants to be. He was still a high school kid. He had some good friendships at school, he was plenty social when it came to that. But I don't think I have ever had a kid as driven as he was. He didn't really pay much attention to the girls or anything that was going to detract him from his basketball journey. Basketball was first for him.

Nationally, among the recruiting gurus, he got off to a slow start. But he was climbing the food chain with the player rankings. From 10th grade to 11th grade, he jumped up. Even back then, the tournaments, the AAU, that was all starting to develop. He was an Adidas player at the time, and Sonny Vaccaro had taken notice of him, had gotten hold of him. That helped get more attention for him, people started recognizing how good he was. He went from a 10th-20th prospect from 10th grade heading into 11th grade, to a Top 5 national prospect in 11th grade heading into 12th grade. And when all was said and done, he was ultimately the best player in the country, a McDonald's All-American, Naismith national player of the year, of course, Pennsylvania player of the year, too.

I used to keep track of this stuff for him, and there was a guy in Florida named Vince Carter who was ranked similarly to Kobe, and another guy, 6-11, named Tim Thomas who was ranked high. Those were pretty big names. But once Kobe got a sniff of what the rankings were, and who was ranked around him, he wanted to go after those people, he wanted to beat them. After we lost in the quarterfinals of the state playoffs in his junior year, I told him that Vince Carter had a broken wrist, and I read somewhere that even with the broken wrist, Vince Carter still led his high school team to a state championship in Florida. I knew that would get him a little bit, he did not want to think of Vince

Carter as better than he. So I would throw in something like that. I knew how to stoke Kobe. I knew how to motivate him, and I knew that was going to light a fire and make him push himself. Once he really started gaining attention, it pushed him to go harder.

The other thing that was going on was, by his senior year, he was scrimmaging with the Sixers at St. Joe's University. That's when he really started breaking out, because the NBA people talk among themselves and all of a sudden, they're hearing about a teenage kid who is playing on a par with pros. The stories of him playing Jerry Stackhouse toe-to-toe, the stories of him dunking on Shawn Bradley, who is 7-foot-6. Everyone was hearing them. At the time, he was playing under the umbrella of John Lucas, who was the 76ers coach. John had kids at Lower Merion, so it was all connected. Once that started happening, I started hearing from Jim Boeheim, and Rick Pitino, and Mike Krzyzewski. Villanova and LaSalle badly wanted him, the local schools, but he was getting too big. I remember a summer league game where Pitino and Krzyzewski and Boeheim were all sitting next to one another watching him. As a coach, that took me aback for a minute, it was a pretty big thrill. But Kobe just sort of handled it; things like that never intimidated him.

He scored 2,883 points in a four-year career, which is the Southeastern Pennsylvania record to this day, ahead of Wilt Chamberlain. He scored 1,047 points in one season, which is kind of unheard of. That was his senior year. When I first had him, we won six games when he was a freshman. But the way things progressed, his career culminated with the 31-3 state championship

season in 1996, when he was a senior. That was our first state championship, and it was a really big deal for our team.

It's been a thrill, and it's been a great 20-year ride for me. I watched the Lakers as close as anybody in the country, I have been able to get to some games and I watch as many games as I can. I was at the 1996 draft on that night at the Meadowlands, and I remember when Charlotte took him and I thought he would be playing for the Hornets. I said to myself, "OK, Charlotte, that is an East Coast team, I can get to see him on occasion, it is not that far." Then 90 minutes later, he is on the Lakers. So, it was not that easy to go watch him play after all. On that draft night, I was not in the inside circle as far as what was going on with that, but it sure worked out well, didn't it?

His final year, being more open with everybody, being willing to accept all the tributes he got—that was good, I think. It was closure for him, and I was not sure how he was going to get that. I am happy with his decision to step away, I think it was the correct decision because obviously his body was breaking down and he couldn't play at a level he wanted to play at. I had a great year personally; one of my players won a national championship for Villanova. I had the thrill of meeting Kobe at halftime in Philadelphia with Dr. J, when they played the Sixers. Myself and Dr. J presented him with a gift. That's not bad, I figured. So, for me, just being able to watch him grow and develop, see him win championships, I am happy now with the closure of it all. Truthfully, I am going to miss it, I really loved watching what the Lakers were doing. The NBA will be different for me now. But I'm very proud of him.

Dave Cowens
Hall of Fame center/forward
Coach

Résumé: Cowens was the fourth overall pick in the 1970 draft by the Celtics and was a dominant big man through the 1970s for Boston, earning eight All-Star selections before abruptly retiring in 1980 (he returned briefly, playing 40 games with Milwaukee in 1982-'83). He was named Rookie of the Year in 1971 and was the MVP of the league in 1972-'73, when he averaged 20.5 points, 16.2 rebounds, and 4.1 assists. He led Boston to championships in 1974 and again in 1976, and finished his career with averages of 17.6 points, 13.6 rebounds, and 3.8 assists. Cowens was briefly a player-coach for the Celtics in 1978-'79 and got into coaching on a more permanent basis after that, first in the Continental Basketball Association, then as an assistant with the Spurs. He was the head coach of the Charlotte Hornets from 1996-'99, and spent a year coaching the Warriors in 2000-'01.

Kobe connection: Cowens was coaching the Hornets when the team drafted Bryant out of high school in 1996, though there is some dispute about how that draft really went down. Bryant claimed that after the draft, Cowens called him and told him the Hornets did not want him, and Kobe said he used that as motivation throughout his career. But Cowens said he did not—and would

*not—call Bryant after the draft, because the Hornets and Lakers
had a draft-day deal arranged between general managers Bob Bass
in Charlotte and Jerry West in L.A. in advance, in which Lakers
big man Vlade Divac would be sent to the Hornets for Bryant.
The facts do bear out Cowens's account, as other teams in that draft
passed on Kobe because his agent at the time, Arn Tellem, had made
clear to front offices around the league that he would only play for
Philadelphia or the Lakers. Cowens later coached the division-rival
Warriors against Bryant in 2000-'01.*

I THINK FROM THE beginning everybody thought he was
going to be a pretty good player. I was coaching the Charlotte
Hornets and we drafted him, and we obviously thought he was
going to be good, but we didn't know how good—he was coming
out of high school, he was a guard, he was not a big guy. All of that
stuff. So you really don't know with a player like that. It is going
to take guys a few years to get their man-body and get used to the
league and stuff like that, so it is a gamble, and it is a risk on a guy
that age. But he was right on schedule, really; by his third year, he
was becoming a dominant player. He did not get the minutes and
the touches in his first couple of years, but he demanded the ball
after that, and that's when he really took off. He carried them ever
since, and he carried them for a long, long time. Even if he has
had trouble staying healthy, I think you have to give him credit
for how long he was able to go out there and play.

I had no problem taking high school kids onto NBA teams, as long as they were ready. I would have had no objection to Kobe being on our team, and even putting him out on the floor if he earned the playing time. I still think they should. I think the reasons they don't get drafted out of high school are more political than anything. I know a lot of coaches, and a lot of people with the league, they did not like the idea of pro scouts in high school gyms. I can understand that, but if someone has talent the way Kobe has talent, why not let them play in the NBA? If a kid wants to make some money, why hold him back? I don't think it is something that hurt Kobe Bryant when you look at his career. If you're good enough, you are going to play in the NBA. I think that is a misperception about that draft, that we did not want him because he was a high school guy. Not at all. We liked him. We just were not sure where he wanted to play; there were a lot of rumors out there about where he wanted to play. We also wanted to bring in some veteran guys.

They had worked a deal. It was already decided we were going to make the trade with the Lakers if everything went as we expected. I think they had another deal, with Atlanta, in place in case something went wrong with ours. They wanted him, and he wanted to play there. Bob Bass was our general manager, and Kobe's agent (Arn Tellem) and Jerry West, they had worked out a deal where Jerry really liked him. Honestly, we liked him, too. I really liked him, it was the first year I took over as coach, though, and we needed a big guy. We got Vlade and we made a deal for Anthony Mason, which was what we needed—we needed some bulk. We had Muggsy Bogues and we had Dell Curry, we had Glen Rice. We had talent in the backcourt, we were looking for big guys.

We got what we wanted out of the deal. Getting Vlade was big for our team, we went from 41 wins to, I think we won 54 games that year. We were a veteran team. Unfortunately, we just did not know how good Kobe was going to be. There was a need for a big guy, so they made the deal happen. It's funny to me, because people might focus on the fact that we traded him, but there were 12 other teams that passed on him. There were good players in that draft—Allen Iverson, Shareef Abdur-Rahim, Ray Allen, Steve Nash. But Kobe turned out to be the best of the bunch, obviously. But there were a lot of teams that did not predict that at the time.

A few years after I was with Charlotte, I was coaching Golden State, and I remember it was a really fun game because Kobe had 51 points and Antawn Jamison matched him for us; he scored 51, too. Antawn was lighting them up, so at some point, as a coach, you just sit back and let them go. Kobe was matching him, and it was pretty cool to see them go back and forth. For me, coaching in that game, you have your sets and you are trying to get your teams into the sets that are going to send the ball to the guy with the hot hand. You don't want to disturb his rhythm. So you're trying to influence the ball into the guy's hands who has got it going on, and you already know what has been working for you. But at the same time, you're trying to figure out how to slow down Kobe, and it just seemed like we had no answers for that. That was amazing; it was something that had not been done in a long, long time (not since 1962, when Elgin Baylor and Wilt Chamberlain each scored 50 in a game). We actually won the game, too, and we did not do too much of that at that time. We won in double-overtime. That must have been great coaching, right?

That just shows how great a scorer a guy like Kobe could be. Most of his career, he played in the triangle offense, and it is a post-up offense that, in an ideal world, ends with the ball going into the hands of someone like Kobe, giving him a post-up opportunity, a guy who can be a playmaker, or a shot-maker, or a finisher himself. A lot like when Phil Jackson had Michael Jordan in Chicago. I think, early in his career, Kobe was figuring out the triangle, but it was almost like he was going to find a way to score whether it was within the offense or outside the offense, it did not matter.

He is an unorthodox kind of scorer; he was that way in the beginning of his career especially. He could shoot, but his form was not that great. He almost had to turn sideways to get everything lined up. He was more comfortable when he was a little off-balance, at least early in his career. It seemed like his elbow wanted to stick out a little bit, so it was almost like he had to turn his shoulder way into the shot. But he made it work. He could make that fadeaway, he had range, he could make free-throws. He could obviously finish drives, and in the open court he was a monster. To be able to cover him on an individual basis was going to be a tall order for any defender, so you had to show him that it was not going to be just one guy, there were going to be other guys waiting for him.

He was just an awesome talent. When I think about players in my era, it is funny, I can't think of one who really matches up with him as far as being a similar comparison. He is a unique talent.

And what probably does not get mentioned enough is that he was a great defender; he took a lot of pride in his defense, and there are plenty of scorers in the NBA who sort of go half-speed on defense. He is such a great competitor that he always wanted to improve on that end of the floor. I was always very impressed with the fact that he would body people up, he would contest, he would rebound, and he was a very tough individual. You have to respect that.

Barry Hecker
Coach/executive

Résumé: Hecker spent more than 40 years in basketball, working as a scout, assistant coach, and personnel director for the Cavaliers, Clippers, and, subsequently, the Grizzlies, while also piling up international experience coaching in China. Hecker was the Clippers' director of scouting from 1986-'94 and moved to the L.A. bench as an assistant to head coach Bill Fitch for four seasons after that. He left the Clippers in 2005 and joined the Memphis Grizzlies' coaching staff under head coach Lionel Hollins.

Kobe connection: Hecker was working with the Clippers in 1996 when he ran a pre-draft workout for Bryant in Los Angeles and was one of the defensive coaches who helped come up with game plans to stop Kobe while in Memphis.

WHEN I WAS coaching with the Clippers in 1996—I had been on the personnel side of things before that—I ran a lot of the workouts for the draft, and that kind of thing. We had him in for a workout, and I remember it was me, Jim Brewer, our head coach Bill Fitch, it was Jeff Weltman, who was in our front office. So we were watching, and I told him to do the Mikan drill; that is the drill where you do the little hook shot on one side of the rim, move over and do the hook shot with your other hand on the other side of the rim, and you go back and forth as long as you can, keeping control of both of your hands the whole time. So Kobe heard me say to do the Mikan drill, and he kind of looked at me and took the ball, and he just dunked it every time. Dunk on the right, dunk on the left, dunk on the right, dunk on the left. Heck with the hook shots, he was dunking, and what was so amazing to me was how quick it was. He just got up and dunked it, then he was already dunking the next one. I could not believe the way he could get up like that. I looked at Brewer, and he looked at me and just said, "Holy sh–, this kid is better than we had heard." Of course, we didn't draft him, there were all the rumors out there and the Clippers at that point were not a very stable organization, probably not the best place for a young high school kid to get started.

The key, when we played the Lakers, was that we knew Kobe was going to get his points and you have got to limit the other guys. Because that was where you would lose the game; you wanted to be able to do the best you could on Kobe one-on-one as long as you could, and then if it looked like he was going to go for 40 or 50 points, well, then you make your adjustment and you bring the double team, you force it out of his hands. But even that was not going to be easy, because everything Kobe did with the basketball was fundamentally sound. Everything was precise, as it was supposed to be, so you could have your defense come, but he was always going to be in the right position to make a play. Not a lot of effort required, did not overdribble, had a great mentality, great intelligence. When I was with Memphis, we had Tony Allen, and we had a good defense in general, so I don't remember him ever really going off like that against us. We could afford to play him one-on-one. That was the way we handled him. When he was in the triangle, the rules for him there were a little different; that offense has different rules from the perspective of the defense.

The difference in the triangle with a guy like Kobe is, in a set offense you know where their scorer is going to be coming from. You've scouted it, you know the play, you know how they're going to do it. He is down in the box, he is going to come up on a pin down, he is going to get a screen and shoot it on the wing, you know the basic things the team is going to do to get him open. In the triangle, everybody is reading and reacting, and it is an offense where everybody is interchangeable. When you scout it, you might be watching it and you want to put the 1 in a certain spot, the 2 in a certain spot, and everybody is where they're supposed to be. It doesn't work like that in a triangle. Everybody is moving around, so you are trying to scout it, but Kobe might be the 5 at one point, then he is the 1 in another. It makes it more difficult, it was a good offense for a guy like him. It made it difficult to defend him, if you had everyone in the offense working on the same page. I mean, he could work out of any set. He would score out of any set. But the triangle, I think that worked better for him than people realized.

The one game I remember in Memphis, it was not the way he scored or anything like that. It was his defense, he just turned it on defensively, and it was incredible. O.J. Mayo was handling the ball for us a lot, and Kobe was just not letting up on him, he was pressuring him the whole way. He just got all over him, and O.J. was having trouble getting the ball up the floor. I think there was the old thing, O.J. was originally hyped up to be the next Kobe Bryant and all that stuff, and he went to USC, he was in L.A. for that year, so I think Kobe might have had some motivation. But it worked. The guy was like a shadow on O.J., he was all over the kid. I think his defense always gets overlooked because when he clamped down on someone, it was over for that guy. If he had the energy to clamp down on you and still keep his offense up, he was a really great two-way player. I felt bad for O.J., to be honest, he was struggling. Kobe was able to turn it up when he wanted to.

That is the thing I think everyone should remember about Kobe. He should be remembered for his whole game. He was a great scorer, of course, but he could pass the ball. He could think the game, he could anticipate plays, he was a good rebounder. And he was a heck of a defensive player. I know people will remember the scoring, and the dunks. Heck, I remember the dunks from the predraft drill we had him run, the Mikan drill. But I hope they remember how hard he worked to be a complete player. That's what he was.

Stu Jackson
Coach/executive

Résumé: Jackson had been an assistant coach on Rick Pitino's staff with the Knicks when he took over the head coaching job in 1989, after Pitino left for Kentucky. After his year-plus stint in New York and a job as Wisconsin's head coach, Jackson became the first person hired by the expansion Vancouver Grizzlies in 1994, as the team's general manager, and stayed in the role through 1997, also serving a half-season as Vancouver's coach. Jackson later moved on to the league office, eventually rising to the level of Executive Vice President of Basketball Operations, where he was in charge of the NBA's competition committee and also oversaw all league discipline, from June 2007-'13.

Kobe connection: The expansion Grizzlies were in their second NBA season when Jackson was tasked with bringing in a player with the No. 3 pick in the draft. Sensing that Bryant had no interest in moving from Philadelphia to the west coast of Canada, Jackson's Grizzlies would draft Shareef Abdur-Rahim from California and let Bryant slide down the draft board. Jackson did have a pretty good sense of how good Kobe would be, as he grew up playing basketball with his father, "Jelly Bean" Bryant. Jackson would go on to become the NBA's head of operations and discipline, and in 2007 he had to suspend Bryant one game for elbowing Marko Jaric in the face shortly after having done the same to Manu Ginobili. (Kobe still disputes the suspension, though Jackson says he could have suspended him for longer.)

REMEMBER WHEN KOBE was coming out in the draft, I was in Vancouver as the general manager. At the time, you could tell from the beginning even as a high school player that he was going to be special; he was headed for greatness. But you might recall in that draft he was only going to play in one of two different places in the league: Philadelphia, where he was from, or for the Lakers. There were rumors that he might go to play in Italy, which some draft picks used as leverage at that time, but I don't think he was going to do any of that. It was the Lakers or Philadelphia, and pretty much everyone knew it; his agent made sure we knew it. Philadelphia had the first pick and was going to take Allen Iverson all the way. So he wound up with the Lakers. I don't know that I would have predicted at that time that, many years later, he'd have accomplished all he did.

Before that 1996 draft, I only saw him on film. As we did our due diligence preparing for that draft, while he was high on our board, just like on everybody's board, we knew ultimately we would not select him. We were an expansion franchise, and when you're an expansion franchise you're trying to build a team with young players That is a key, of course, and you have to build through the draft. You're running the risk of making a draft choice that would not be the best fit. We all knew that Kobe wanted to play in a couple of places, so he was not going to be a fit for us. He was really young, and he knew what he wanted. If we had taken him, I don't know how he would have reacted, but at least initially it would not have been good. Maybe he would have played in Vancouver, but there was enough talk that he was only going to play for those two teams that you could not risk making that pick.

We played the Lakers that year, after I took over the coaching job. He was a young, gangly 18-year-old. But you certainly saw, like you can see in some players of that age, you can see they have talent. That was obvious. A lot of times with players that age, what you can't tell is whether or not that talent would translate into greatness. But what impressed me about Kobe at that very early age was that his competitiveness was there, his competitiveness was very high, the belief in himself. He had confidence in what he could do, and he was very willing to take risks and try things on the floor that most players were not capable of trying. The first time I coached against him, he did not play much at all (only five minutes), and I knew that, when he wanted to go to the Lakers before the draft, he was not expecting to be on the bench so much. I think he started the last game we played against them and had a really good game (20 points, eight rebounds). I had a pretty good feeling it was going to work out there. Because of his talent level, you could see, it was extraordinary. Even just in warmups, you would peek over at him because he might do something worth seeing.

I played against his father in high school. I am from Reading, Pa., so I played in Philadelphia summer leagues in the summer. It was the Sonny Hill League, the Narberth Summer League, and Jelly Bean (Bryant) was in both of those leagues, so I got to play against Kobe's dad quite a bit in those leagues. Knowing that, it is funny to think about, knowing how different he was from his father as a player—his father was 6-9, had the ability to play in the forward spot, he could be a power forward, but Jelly Bean was a guy who had perimeter skills. He had the ability to put the ball on the floor, had the ability to pass and make plays. Obviously, he played in the league for a while, and played for the Sixers, like all of us at that time wanted to do. He had a lot of talent. Jelly Bean was a great runner at his size, he had great leaping ability, great passing ability, so you could say that Kobe acquired some of his skills from his father. He just was not as long and big as his father. Kobe was a lot more athletic, obviously. But if you knew Jelly Bean and watched him play, or played against him, you would not be surprised that he would be the father of a great player.

What separated Kobe in general from other players was that work ethic, and in the draft you just can't see that. Work ethic in a player comes in stages. As a franchise, you want to make the determination that he has a work ethic that will propel him to make him better individually, in the short term. That you can determine throughout the process of your investigation in the draft by talking to his coaches or opposing coaches, or whoever you might find for that level of due diligence. What you don't know is how players' work ethic will translate as the years go on and they become more experienced professionals. You saw it with Michael Jordan and the way he committed himself to making himself better as he aged. The same thing happened with Kobe. Yes, he worked very hard as a young player to make himself better, to make himself an All-Star player. But what was extraordinary about Kobe, like Michael, was that as he started to age, you saw his work ethic change. It was exponential.

He committed himself to continually changing his body, whether it was making himself stronger, making himself quicker, whether it was to make himself a better shooter over the course of a game or a season, or to prepare himself to minimize the risk of injury or to take on the minutes required to carry the team in May and June. That requires a really different kind of work ethic from NBA players who play for a long, long time. Because what happens is, guys that last that long, or who are very young players, they end up getting their second contract, that really big payday, and you don't know what's going to happen from there. There are guys who love the game so much they would work on it and spend all that time in the gym even if they were not making that kind of money. Those guys are rare, and they're special. Kobe was as much that kind of player as anyone.

Even though I knew his dad, Kobe and I were never close or anything beyond saying hello. He definitely showed more of himself in his final year, which was great. But it is hard when you are the guy who does discipline, you don't get to know the guys you are policing. Personally, Kobe did not engage with me that way. I think he is still angry at me for suspending him for hitting Ginobili and Jaric. I never got to see the friendlier part of him. I can't say I blame him! But no, knowing his father and his father's personality, I was not surprised to see him over the course of his final year in the league let his personality show a little bit. I thought that was great; his father is a really good guy, so it was good to see that. But to say he was unhappy with me for suspending him would be too light a word; he was serious. But those two hits were as hard hits as I ever reviewed in my time with the league. He stopped doing it after that.

When I think about him, I don't know what other superlatives you could add to his career. The number of championships he has won, the MVPs, the Finals MVP. But the best thing you can say about him is he is one of the ten best players of all time ever to play the game. That is a big thing to say, and I think anyone would agree that Kobe is at least in the Top 10 in history.

Antonio Harvey
Power forward/broadcaster

Résumé: Harvey played eight seasons in the NBA, including starting his career with the Lakers for two years. He left for Vancouver as part of the expansion draft just before Kobe Bryant entered the league, but he played for Lakers coach Del Harris, the same coach

*Bryant had to start his career. Harvey was a role player who aver-
aged 3.0 points in 187 career NBA games, suiting up for six different teams and also spending two years playing in Europe. He served
as the Portland Trailblazers' color commentator for 11 seasons.*

Kobe connection: *Harvey took the floor against Bryant four times
in the regular season during his career, and Kobe Lakers won three
of them. But it was a series in the postseason that was the most
significant—the famed 2001 Western Conference finals, in which
Bryant and the Lakers built a 3-1 series lead before the Blazers
fought back to force a Game 7 and take a 16-point lead in the
second half at the Staples Center. But Kobe scored 25 points with
11 rebounds and seven assists, and teammate Shaquille O'Neal
scored 18, as the Lakers capped a comeback with an alley-oop from
Bryant to O'Neal. Long before that, though, the game that stands
out for Harvey is a summer league game that took place in 1996.*

WHEN KOBE CAME in, I had already been with the Lakers, and really that coaching staff, the Del Harris coaching staff, had been my coaching staff before I was taken in the
expansion draft by the Grizzlies. I knew the coaches for the
Lakers very well from my time there, and I had good relationships with them all; they would do favors for me if they could,
and vice versa. I remember Larry Drew was still an assistant
with that Lakers team. When the summer league started that

season in 1996, Larry called me over to the side and asked me to do him a favor. He said, "We've got this rookie, he doesn't understand what his place is, he is cocky. He thinks he knows it all, he thinks he knows what is going on. I need you to check him a little bit, in the game. Make sure he knows his place, you know."

I said, "Well all right, OK." I liked that kind of stuff. Playing physical, that was right up my alley. Everyone knew about Kobe already at that point, of course. But if you had already been in the league, you did not want there to be rookies who got ahead of themselves, and that was how older guys looked at it. He came right from high school, and he needed to be checked a little bit. He had already played a summer league game before that, he scored 30-something points, and everyone was talking about him. So as a veteran, an older guy, I thought, OK, I can do that.

Summer league comes, it is in Long Beach at the Pyramid, everyone in and around L.A. was all excited and ready to see this new young guy come in. Everybody wants to see Kobe. And I just want to help out Larry. Kobe gets the ball and he is facing me, and I wanted to give him a hit or two, like Larry said. So, I would reach in, and he'd be gone. I'd try to body him and he would slide by me, no contact. I couldn't check him. Like, his athleticism was so off the charts that I was there trying to hit him, and I ended up just missing him. Larry is looking at me like, "Come on!" but I did not know what to tell him; the guy wouldn't let me hit him. Larrry was frustrated, so finally I turned and said to Larry, "I'm trying, man, but he's too quick!" He was so athletic at that age, and he had such good instincts, you could not really even make contact with him. It was the instincts, he just could see what everyone was doing out there.

But the thing I remember best was the 1999-2000 Western Conference finals, the series that everyone always talks about. It was a great series, and it was interesting to watch him because we had a very good game plan, and he really struggled for a big part of that series. We are facing them, and they ended up beating us in that series. But we had a game plan where we were going to try to exploit one of Kobe's big weaknesses, and that was his defense in the post. That was Mike Dunleavy's plan. We just kept sending our guards in, so Steve Smith posted him up, Bonzi Wells posted him up, Stacey Augmon posted him up. We took him down into the post over and over. That really wore him out, it frustrated him, it slowed the game down, it gave us an advantage. The first five games, he had I think one game where he went over 20 points. (Bryant's totals in the first five games were 13, 12, 25, 18, and 17 points.) Our guards wore him out by backing him down in that post.

Well, to show you the kind of player Kobe Bryant was, he went home that summer and he came back twenty pounds heavier. It was like he just added a layer of muscle, in one summer. It was because of what Bonzi and Steve and those guys did to him in the playoffs. He was not going to let himself be pushed around in the post anymore. The added strength changed that forever; you could not post him up anymore. They won a championship in that season, they beat us and went and beat Indiana, but that was not good enough for him. I think in his mind he was still worrying about the number of times we took him into the post and how he needed to put a stop to it. He didn't want any weaknesses showing. That speaks to the type of player he was, the type of star he was. You might get me once on something like that, you might exploit me on that when I am not expecting it, but you won't get me twice.

He was different that way. Kobe was not a talker, he was not a guy who was going to tell you what he was thinking. Michael Jordan, he would put it in your face that he was the greatest player ever. He loved that, he loved telling you that. Kobe did it different. He knew he was the greatest player ever, but he dared you to try to prove otherwise. You were going to have to take that title from him, but he was not going to give it. He's not like anybody else, maybe just Mike—they're the only two guys I came across cut from that same cloth. I know we compare Michael and Kobe; it is natural, it is what we do. I think those guys, they are just different in the way they approach the game, different from just about every athlete. They were different in their approach, but their dedication, to me, it seemed to be the same.

I had a chance to talk with Kobe for a while in Portland at the end, during his last year when the Lakers were playing the Blazers. I had never really had that chance, because he sort of kept everyone at a distance, he did that everywhere. And honestly, I hated him. I hated him his entire career. I think he wanted that, he didn't care if guys like me hated him. But once I talked with him, once I saw he was not the Kobe I thought I knew, the guy who was killing us with daggers, I could appreciate what he had done, how he had sacrificed to play the game. It changed my view of him completely. He's really a good guy.

I think that people should remember—and I tell this to my kids—when he went down with that Achilles tear, then walked back on the floor and shot his free throws, then walked back to the bench, that was amazing. Dealing with the pain, walking out there and finishing your job. With a torn Achilles. You see guys go down with an Achilles and they don't get up. They have to be carried off the court. You see that all the time with guys, they get hurt and they're bringing out a stretcher for a sprained ankle. Kobe would not let anyone help him, he wanted to walk. I remember watching that and I thought no way he tore his Achilles because he wouldn't have been walking. And the next day, the news comes out, torn Achilles. That was amazing, because that is a level of dedication that 99.999 percent of athletes would never have. I still hated him then, but I sure respected him.

Cedric Ceballos
Forward

Regular Season	Games	Wins	Losses	Win %	Field Goal %	PPG	Points (High)	RPG	APG	SPG
Bryant	5	4	1	0.80	0.461	19.2	25 (twice)	7.6	3.6	1.4
Ceballos	5	1	4	0.20	0.486	11.2	16 (4/18/00)	6	0.6	0.8

Résumé: Ceballos played for 11 NBA seasons, suiting up for the Suns, Lakers, Mavericks, and Heat. He averaged 14.3 points playing in 609 NBA games, was a career 50.0 percent in shooting, and made the Western Conference All-Star team in 1995 while playing in L.A. He had a breakout season in 1992-'93, his third year in the NBA, but he injured his knee in the Western Conference finals and was unable to play in the Finals showdown with the Bulls—an injury many in Phoenix feel cost them that year's championship. Ceballos, who has since embarked on a successful radio career, retired in 2001.

Kobe connection: *Ceballos was one of Bryant's original teammates with the Lakers, and though Ceballos did not stick around for long after Kobe was drafted, he did play an important two-part role in Bryant's early career. For one thing, he helped Kobe get adjusted to the NBA during his first few months of training camp and the exhibition season. Also, Ceballos was the primary piece used to bring disgruntled Suns forward Robert Horry to the Lakers in a trade. Horry, of course, would go on to be one of the most-recognized makers of big shots in the league's recent history, particularly for the Lakers, which helped to take away the sting of the loss of Ceballos. To cap off his connection with Bryant, Ceballos was among the former Lakers invited to the Staples Center for Kobe's final game.*

WHEN KOBE WAS a rookie, he was in a much different situation than most rookies, obviously. He was in a tough position because he had a lot of hype. Everybody had heard about him, but everybody knew at his age he was not going to play, not on a veteran team like the Lakers. But then, for one thing, he got hurt before training camp, at Venice Beach. So when we went to camp in Hawaii, he was not going through full contact. We also did not really get to haze him quite as much, getting doughnuts and carrying bags and that sort of thing. I mean, there was some of that, but most of it happens during the preseason, and he was hurt. Shaq did have him do some goofy things, like bust a freestyle rap for all of us. For the most part, though, we did not have a lot of established veterans who had been there. Byron Scott was the only one with stripes, as we say, a veteran who earned the right to do that kind of thing. But Byron was 35 and he was already thinking about getting into coaching, so he was not going to get into that hazing kind of stuff. It wasn't really Kobe's kind of thing; like I said, he was different. Most rookies want the approval of the veterans. He never really was that way.

But what made me think Kobe was really different was that, before camp, before he got hurt, he would come and practice with other pros in L.A. in the morning, then he would go to UCLA and practice with those guys after that. Then he would turn around and go to Palisades High School, and he would practice there. He was putting himself through three practices a day, and practicing against every level of player. It was phenomenal that he was doing that. A lot of guys thought no way he should be practicing that much, but he was 17. He just loved playing basketball, and it did not matter to him who he was playing against. Let him practice all he wants.

He came in and he did not conduct himself like he was a 17-year-old kid. I think some of that came from his father; he had a certain level of knowledge of what to expect. I think he expected there to be some jealousy or resentment because he was basically a freshman in college playing with us, and no one on our team had ever had a teammate quite like him. There was some jealousy, but not too much. He came in confident, he knew what jokes to make, what jokes not to make. I don't want to say he had it all figured out. He didn't. I think he had a lot of knowledge, he had lived all over the world, but he did need a little bit more regular old common sense. I mean, I remember one morning coming in, and he was sitting in his car listening to rap albums outside our place. He had a $100,000 car, and we were in Inglewood, which wasn't the safest place at that time, and here is Kobe Bryant, in his Los Angeles Lakers uniform, listening to rap albums with the volume turned up. I had to tell him, you know, Kobe, how about you not do that anymore? That's not too safe.

I think he was frustrated in the beginning because he was not playing, and he thought he should be. He should have been playing more, really. Del Harris was just not a rookie coach. He was an old-school guy; he didn't want to play him much, and in fairness to Del, he was under pressure. He had to win, and he did not think he could do that with a 17-year-old kid. The word had to come down from Jerry West that Kobe should start playing some. But it was like, the more he was not playing once the season started, the more he wanted to show everyone what he could do, including Del, including all of us who were his teammates. In practice, he would just make these unbelievable attempts. We were working on half-court offense one time, and the bench was going against the starters, so Shaq was in the middle for the starters and Kobe got the ball on a cut across the lane. Kobe went in and tried a 360-dunk on Shaq. He didn't make it, but that took some guts, trying to dunk on the most dominant big man in the league, even in practice. And not only that, but trying to pull off a 360 to do it.

That kind of thing only ticked off Del Harris even more. Kobe was always trying these unbelievable attempts in practices, and Del would get mad and tell him to take the easy shot and make the easy play. But he was a rookie who was not playing. He wanted to make the spectacular play. He was trying to prove himself to Del, like, "I can do this, but you are still not going to play me?" We nicknamed him Showboat, because he was always trying to show off these crazy moves all the time. But I will say that he played hard all the time in practice. There was never a day that he was down or sick or not at practice. And he lit up like a firecracker when it came time to scrimmage.

Off the court, though, I don't know how happy he was. It's hard to imagine being that age and being thrown into a pro team like that, in Los Angeles. I have always said, Kobe was never there to make friends, he never played basketball to make friends. That was clear from the beginning. We would all say we are going out, and he would just ignore it. Even just to walk around the mall somewhere, he wouldn't go. We'd say we're going to dinner, you know, that is part of being a team, the social side of it. But he was not interested in that. Maybe his dad had already groomed him, and I can understand it now—teammates are always going to come and go, but you have got to focus on yourself. He did not want to go to the clubs, he did not even want to go to movies or dinner. He had a lot of CDs, he liked that, he would take them along and just listen to them in his room. He was like the opposite of Magic Johnson. Magic was everybody's buddy. He would show up at your kid's birthday or the barbeque your uncle is having. Kobe went the other way. I think he wanted to stay on the edge, be by himself.

It is funny to think of how far he went, from when he was that young guy to when he finally retired. Honestly, I knew he would be a star, like a celebrity star, and I knew that from Jump Street. He was just too good at that young age. I figured he would have been dangerous even without Shaq, but playing with Shaq you knew they were going to win at least one championship. You could see that their games would work well together, until they let their egos get in the way. What I did not think was that he could not do that without Shaq, that he could have won those championships with Pau Gasol, Lamar Odom. But he just continued to carry that team.

When he announced his retirement, I was looking for tickets. I wanted to try to go to some of his last games, though not necessarily the last one. I saw the date, and I thought it would be better to watch it than to be there. But then they announced that they wanted all his former teammates to be there for his final game. That, for me, was something I will never forget, just being there. When they played that video of him growing up, all that stuff, it was so well done, that place was as loud as it could be. I never heard that place like that. It was a textbook story. And then he went out and had 60. I said before the game that it would be sweet if he had 50 points. And that's Kobe for you—you expect 50, but I am going to give you 10 more. 60 points. What a great way to finish.

Eddie Johnson
Small forward/shooting guard

Regular Season	Games	Wins	Losses	Win %	Field Goal %	PPG	Points (High)	RPG	APG	SPG
Bryant	4	2	2	0.50	0.472	18	27 (12/12/97)	3.3	0.5	1.5
Johnson	4	2	2	0.50	0.379	6.5	15 (3/7/97)	2.3	1	0.3

Résumé: Johnson was an outstanding reserve player for most of his career and won the league's Sixth Man of the Year Award in 1989. He averaged 21.5 points off the bench that year, making nearly 50 percent of his shots. In all, Johnson played 18 seasons, mostly with the Kings, for whom he played six years, both in Sacramento and Kansas City. Johnson's career numbers are impressive:16.0 points, 4.0 rebounds, and 47.2 percent shooting—and, in fact, he holds the record for most career points scored (19,202) without playing in an All-Star game. Johnson has gotten into radio broadcasting since retiring from basketball.

Kobe connection: Johnson was already nearing the NBA's exit when Bryant was brought into the league by the Lakers in 1996, but Johnson did face the very young version of Kobe four times on his way out. Johnson scored 15 points in the first meeting of the pair, to just eight for Bryant, but the 19-year-old Kobe came back in December of 1997 and scored 27 points on Johnson's Rockets in only 26 minutes of action. It was obvious to Johnson that Bryant had talent even early in his career, but what struck Johnson most was Kobe's curiosity about the nature of the game.

MY MEMORY OF him was his rookie year; it was one of my last years playing. I was playing for the Houston Rockets, and he was not getting a ton of time back then. They had Eddie Jones at that time, and they were giving all the minutes at that spot to him. It was late in the year, in March, and they put him in the game late, and someone was shooting free throws. So we were at the other end, standing there, and the only reason I remember this now is because of all the stories I heard from other players over the course of his career, that he would always seek advice. At the time, I did not know he was like that. But at the very beginning he was there, and we were talking during those free throws. I didn't know it was a ritual for him.

For me, it is always surprising to me when a young player knows who you are. It is kind of crazy, but realistically a lot of young guys don't know half the players on the opposing team. So we were standing there and he said to me, "Eddie . . . " And I think I ignored him because I figured he did not know me and he was talking to somebody else or something. I was surprised right there, he knew who I was. We started talking, I asked him how his first year was going, and he said, "Man, it's a struggle, it's a struggle. Dude won't play me. I can play right now. I don't know why he won't play me." I looked at him as he was saying this to me, and honestly, you could see the pain in his face as he was saying that.

I have gotten into conversations with young players before, I have talked with them, and, yeah, they all think they should be playing 40 minutes and all of that. They don't want your help, they just want to talk. But when I talked to Kobe, I will never forget, I really believed him. It really stuck out, because the way he said it to me was not just complaining or whining, it was this certainty that Del Harris did not know what he was doing. It was not disrespectful, it was more like, "I'm in jail and this guy won't let me out." And he wanted some advice from me, like maybe I could help him get out of jail or at least help him deal with it.

I wanted to give him the best answer I could give him, because he was sincere. It was like he was asking me to tell him something that would make him feel better about all of it. And I had heard and seen that he was going to be a different kind of player, that he was going to be a special player. I did not know how special, but I knew he was not going to be coming off the bench for long. So I told him that. If that greatness is there, it is not going to stay on the bench for long. And I looked at him and just said, "Kobe, be patient. Just be patient." I think it was the best thing I could have told him, it was probably the one thing he needed at the time. I don't think he had a lot of patience at that time, or now really. But I wanted him to know, greatness will win out. Just to be able to know he was going to get his chance.

The truth is, I think even though he was young and maybe some guys saw him as a little cocky, we all heard about him.

I know I heard about him in that gossipy dungeon of the NBA. We all talk, and we all heard stories about how different this guy was. I heard rumors of guys with the Lakers complaining about him. "Man, this guy doesn't want to go out with anybody," "He doesn't want to go to the club, or hang out," "He's a loner," "He's always in the gym or in his room."

I was in my late 30s, and I was in a position where if I could have talked to myself when I was 18 or 19, I would say, "Stay in your room, go to the gym, don't go out, work on your game." I was hearing all this stuff, and thinking that these guys were complaining but they had it backwards. I was saying, "Wait, this kid has it figured out. He is doing what he is supposed to do." Some of his teammates took it as being he doesn't want to be one of them, he wants to be above them, he doesn't have any swag, he doesn't want to be one of us. But I thought, no, he is just dedicated. He knows at age 18 what most of us don't figure out until we are in our 30s. He has his head on straight. That grabbed my attention about him. When I would see him on the court, making plays and executing, I would think, that is no accident. He is putting in the work, like all of us should be doing.

I was never surprised by what I saw him accomplish, because he really had that plethora game, the guy who could do everything—the midrange game, could shoot the three, could drive on you. We don't have that anymore. Now the guys who come in on the perimeter, they are in love with the three, and they are so in love with the three that they're not developing other parts of their game. I don't think we'll ever see that in the NBA again, not with the way the game is set up now. Kobe was a guy who could get his shot anywhere he was on the floor. He was a guy who had moves in the post, had moves in the mid-range game, where he could get a good shot for himself. You go back and watch him in the prime of his career, and what made him great was not his dunks or his fast-break plays or three-pointers; it was just him, breaking down a guy from 18 feet and rising up for a good look, and knocking it down.

That's Kobe. I don't think we will see that again.

PART 2:
THE SHAQ-AND-KOBE YEARS

"**I GOT THE YOUNG,** high-jumping, shooting-in-your-face, not-passing Kobe. That is probably the scariest Kobe of all. We had to deal with Shaq, too, no question. But at that time, there was no Shaq without Kobe." –*Chris Webber*

FOR A WHILE, at least, it was great. A juggernaut had arrived in Lakerland.

It was exactly what Lakers honcho Jerry West envisioned when he first began pulling the strings in the offseason of 1996, the strings that brought in both Kobe Bryant and Shaquille O'Neal, together. The brute force of O'Neal and his 300-plus-pound frame knocking around bodies on the interior. The precision midrange game and attack mentality of Bryant on the perimeter. On a personal level, O'Neal even took to calling Kobe "Little Brother," and in the wake of Bryant's four air balls in the 1997 playoffs, it was O'Neal who comforted Bryant and told him that all he needed to do was to take—and make—those same shots next year, without fear.

By Bryant's third season, when it was clear he should be a starter, the Lakers began to accommodate him. They dealt away Eddie Jones in March 1999 and installed Bryant in the starting lineup, where he would remain, coming off the bench only five times in the next 18 years of his career. Bryant averaged 19.9 points that year, and more good news came for him when Harris was finally fired. The Lakers still lost disappointingly to end that season, being swept out of the post-lockout playoffs by the Spurs. But changes were afoot, and in the offseason, the Lakers brought in former Bulls coach Phil Jackson, who had led Chicago to six NBA trophies in the previous decade, in hopes of pushing the team into the elite of the NBA. When Jackson arrived in Los Angeles, he brought with him the same triangle offense, developed by assistant coach Tex Winter, that he had used to emphasize Michael Jordan with the Bulls and help him be a dominant force throughout the postseason. Considering Bryant's notable affinity for Jordan and his style of play, this was a happy turn of events for Kobe.

Jackson also brought a master motivator's mentality, and excelled at organizing a team and getting each part of it functioning correctly, whether stars like Bryant and O'Neal or role players like Derek Fisher and Brian Shaw. On his arrival in Los Angeles, Jackson said, "I believe they are a group of players who want to get there but don't know quite how." Jackson would show them. And so the Lakers began to thrive, and where they had previously choked away postseason chances, often in embarrassing fashion, they now seized those chances instead. They beat Portland in a taut seven-game series in the 2000 playoffs, then finished by beating the Pacers in the Finals to win their first Kobe-Shaq championship. They cruised through the 2001 playoffs with a dominating performance, losing only one game and beating Philadelphia in the Finals to win their second straight trophy.

They pulled off a grueling win in a controversial 2002 Western Conference Finals against the Kings, one that found the Lakers behind, 3-2, in the series and required them to go to overtime of the seventh game to finally get the win and send them to a third straight Finals. Once there, the Lakers dismantled the Nets with ease, registering a four-game sweep.

But even as everything was falling into place on the court, rumblings were developing off it. Both Bryant and O'Neal felt that they should be No. 1 options in the Lakers' offense. As Jackson saw it, the ideal would be for O'Neal to wear down opponents during the game's first three quarters, allowing Bryant to step in and finish off games in the fourth. Bryant did not see himself as a one-quarter player, though. He did not want to be O'Neal's relief pitcher. O'Neal knew that, with his size, he was indispensable, and in the team hierarchy that would win out against a perimeter guy like Bryant. But Bryant would spend his entire offseason training and honing his game, showing up for camp ready to play—while O'Neal would routinely arrive out of shape, saying he could play his way back into good condition as the season progressed. Bryant grew resentful of the lack of work O'Neal put in, and resentful of the fact that he was being asked to sacrifice his game, to mold it around O'Neal.

The Spurs, adding young international players Manu Ginobili and Tony Parker, were a much-improved team in 2002-'03 and knocked off the Lakers in the West semifinals, halting the L.A. dynasty. The Lakers looked set to recover, especially after the signings of future Hall of Famers Gary Payton and Karl Malone to join O'Neal and Bryant. The influence of the old-head star veterans and the creation of this Lakers super team seemed to be enough to mend the Bryant-O'Neal rift. That was the hope, at least. But for the Lakers, the worst was yet to come.

In the summer of 2003, Bryant suffered a personal low point when he was arrested and charged with sexual assault while he was staying at a resort hotel in Colorado. The charge was later dropped, but for a player whose only real public squabble was his back-and-forth with O'Neal and complaints that he was a ball hog on the floor, Bryant was for the first time thrown into personal conflict and painted as a villain. But the seriousness of the arrest did not temper his battle with O'Neal—rather, the more besieged Bryant appeared to be by his legal issues, the more his tiff with O'Neal turned into a full-scale war. The Lakers may have titillated fans and media by signing a pair of future Hall of Famers, Karl Malone and Gary Payton, but the attention that came with their addition only brought another heap of attention on top of Bryant's legal troubles, a knee problem he was dealing with, and the rift with O'Neal. In the Lakers' training camp in Hawaii, while Bryant was back in Colorado, O'Neal told reporters, "The full team is here."

Just before the start of the season, Bryant did an interview with Jim Gray in which he bashed O'Neal's leadership credentials, saying, "Leaders don't beg for a contract extension . . . in the media." He added that if O'Neal were a leader, he would stop "coming into camp fat and out of shape." Bryant also said that, if he decided to leave the Lakers in free agency, it would be because of "Shaq's childlike selfishness and jealousy."

Entering the 2003-'04 season, the Lakers had crossed a bridge with Shaq and Kobe. Then the Lakers were left to watch the two burn that bridge. "That's something I think every basketball fan will always wonder," ESPN analyst Jalen Rose said. "What if they had not fought like that, or what if they put it aside and just played? How many rings would they have won?"

Baron Davis

Guard

Regular Season	Games	Wins	Losses	Win %	Field Goal %	PPG	Points (High)	RPG	APG	SPG
Bryant	29	22	7	0.76	0.408	28.1	44 (2/2/01)	6.8	4.8	1.6
Davis	29	7	22	0.24	0.389	16.1	30 (twice)	3.6	6.8	2.3

Résumé: Davis grew up in Los Angeles and went to UCLA, where he suffered an ACL injury but still was good enough to go No. 3 in the draft to the Hornets in 1999. Davis did struggle with his health in the NBA, but he played 13 seasons, made two All-Star appearances, and averaged 16.1 points and 7.2 assists over the course of his career. He had his most memorable period in the NBA in 2005, after he was traded from New Orleans to the Warriors at the trade deadline, and proceeded to help lead Golden State to a stunning upset of the top-seeded Mavericks in the opening round of the playoffs.

Kobe connection: As a fellow L.A. guy, Davis made an early connection with Bryant, who frequently worked out at the gym at UCLA and gave Davis the opportunity to play him one-on-one during one afternoon. The two remained friendly throughout their NBA careers, and though they saw each other often, Davis's teams clearly could not decipher how to defend Bryant, who went 22-7 all-time against Davis's clubs and averaged 28.1 points in those games.

MY FAVORITE MEMORY with Kobe goes all the way back to college. We wound up playing one-on-one during practice while I was hurt. I hurt my knee while I was a freshman at UCLA. I was doing my rehab, and it was during the NBA lockout. I was not fully cleared to practice, but we were having practice at UCLA, so I was there. I had to sort of stay off to the side. So I am watching and doing rehab and I look up, and Kobe Bryant walks into the gym. He did not say anything to anybody, he just started working out, working on his shot over on the other court. He would do that even during the season sometimes, but he was doing it more during the lockout.

I was just sitting there, so I went over to him and asked him if he needed me to rebound for him. He said yeah and he shot a little more, but then he asked me if I wanted to play one-on-one. The team was practicing, I was not supposed to be out there because of my knee, but we were on the next court and I did not think anyone could see us. I mean, I was not cleared to play one-on-one against my teammates, let alone against Kobe Bryant. But I was not going to say no. It's Kobe Bryant; what kid in college is not going to say yes to that? We started playing these games of one-on-one, and next thing I know, I am already down, 3-0, three games to none. He definitely got me; he was not going light on me. I think I won a couple of games there, but that was it. Mostly, I just remember that he kicked my butt. And then I looked over and my teammates must have gotten a look at what was going on, because they were all watching me. They were watching me lose. I think I might have won two games, maybe.

But that was big for me personally. It was a crazy experience. For him, in his history, he was really just starting at that point, he was just getting to be big. I was still in college, a sophomore, going through what I was going through at UCLA. For me, it was always like a point where I realized, "Man, this is Kobe Bryant. If I can do this, if I can play him one-on-one with my knee feeling like this, then I know I can play in the NBA." He probably had no idea who I was at that time, but it affected me. I still remember it now.

Kobe was just the ultimate competitor and the ultimate talent. He had all the offensive weapons that he was gifted and blessed with. For a while in some of the games I played against him, in the 2000s, he was not just gifted athletically, but he had gotten to that point where he was smart, too. He had such a high basketball IQ, and he could break you down not only with what he was doing, but with the way he was thinking. I saw a lot of guys, guys who were good defenders, trying to guard him, and you try to stay in front of him, but he is going to see one small thing the guy is doing—his feet are positioned wrong or something like that—and he can exploit it. Because he has seen it all, and he can figure out how to expose a weakness. He had the best offensive weaponry of anyone I have ever seen.

Now, he also showed up and played at the Drew League, and that is a special league to me, a league in L.A. near where I grew up, and it has gotten big. It usually has some NBA players coming in and playing some. It is a great, high-level rec league that I have been involved with since I was a kid. But for Kobe to play, that was huge for us. And I will always appreciate Kobe because he came down to the Drew and played there. I will always have a special spot for him, because the league is like, no frills, it is just L.A. people who love basketball. Someone of Kobe's stature does not have to go down and play there. But Kobe came one year, in 2011, and he put on a show. James Harden, who is from L.A., as well, he was playing, too, and he was on the other team. And they went at each other. I mean, this is where you see how competitive Kobe is, because this was not a game on national TV; this was a few hundred people in a gym. And it was on a Tuesday, and we don't usually even play Drew League games on a Tuesday. But he had called and contacted (Drew League head) Dino Smiley, and he really wanted to do all he could to make it happen. He did.

And the game was cool. I mean, he really entertained everyone; people still talk about it, years later. Dino tried to keep it a secret that he was going to play, but everyone knew and word got around, so it was packed. He and James Harden went back and forth, I think they both scored more than 40 points each. But it was down to the end and Kobe made a shot to win it, a game-winner, and he just stood with his arms up and everybody rushed to him, all the crowd. It was a great moment, because really, the Drew League is all about L.A. basketball, and no one is more about L.A. basketball than Kobe Bryant. He has continued to come back to the Drew; he has continued to support the Drew since that game. I think it meant something to him.

He will always be the No. 1 player as far as L.A. is concerned. The Lakers struggled at the end of his career, he struggled to play, struggled to stay healthy, but it does not matter. He is still the No. 1 guy.

Blue Edwards
Forward/guard

Regular Season	Games	Wins	Losses	Win %	Field Goal %	PPG	Points (High)	RPG	APG	SPG
Bryant	8	8	0	1.00	0.462	11.8	20 (3/27/97)	2.6	2.4	0.9
Edwards	8	0	8	0	0.435	8.9	20 (4/8/98)	3.6	2.8	1

Résumé: Edwards was a productive shooting guard for ten NBA seasons, originally selected by Utah out of East Carolina. With the Jazz for three seasons, he averaged 12.6 points per game in his final year with Utah before he was traded to Milwaukee, as the Jazz sought to ease their glut of wing players and find a good backup for John Stockton (Jay Humphries of the Bucks was thought to be that point guard). Edwards went to the Celtics before returning to the Jazz for a half-season, ultimately landing in Vancouver as an expansion draft player in 1995, the last player the Grizzlies picked. He led the Grizzlies in total scoring in their initial season, though, and recorded the franchise's first triple-double.

Kobe connection: Edwards faced off against Kobe eight times in his career, and the Lakers won all eight games. In the final meetings between the two, Bryant's second season in the NBA, they had some significant exchanges, with Edwards outscoring Kobe, 15-13, in one meeting and again outscoring him, 20-14, in their final matchup in 1997. Even so, Bryant left his impression on Edwards.

WHAT I REMEMBER was just seeing this young, athletically gifted player who had what they call a "live body"—there was an electricity about him where he was going to make things happen. He was, even when he was young, ultra-competitive; he wanted to attack you, he was creative and somewhat unpredictable. I was a Lakers fan when I was growing up, so I was always hyped to play them. And when we got to play against Kobe, there was already this buzz around him. You could sense that there was something different about him: the way he carried himself, the look he had in his eye, the look on his face, the way he went about the pregame warmup, how serious he was, and things like that.

You could line up ten players, and if Kobe Bryant was in the line there would be something that would draw you to him, something that would make him stand out and make him distinctive. Even though he was so young, it was not like we were against him. I know for me personally, there was no sense of being out to get him or jealousy, or anything like that. But that was the era where high school kids were coming into the league, and Kevin Garnett had been in the previous year, he was drafted out of high school. I had the same experience with both of those guys, with KG and Kobe. With those guys, you see a young guy guarding you, a teenager, and you want to go at them. I did that to KG. I did that to Kobe, trying to attack him, trying to make sure he had to keep up with me, saying, "Young fella can't guard me," and that kind of thing. Try to get in their heads.

But what impressed me about Kobe, and Garnett was the same way, is that he came right back at me. He tried to score, too. Garnett was an intense, fierce competitor, he would talk right back to you. Kobe approached it a different way, though; he did not come back at you with the same force, he came back at you skillfully. He didn't back down, but he was going to slice you up like a surgeon rather than hit you with a sledgehammer like Kevin Garnett. You could be faced up with Kobe and think you have him locked up—this happened to me more than once—but he could put one move on you, two moves, and be by you. I can remember thinking it was a fluke, he got lucky. But then he'd do it again, and another time, and you would realize, it's no fluke. He's just good like that. Fortunately, (Lakers coach) Del Harris would get him out of the game by then, so you would not have to deal with it too much. But, yeah, he should have been playing more, I would say.

With Kobe, it was obvious that he was a different kind of kid. You can see when a person is focused on the game when you see them in the pregame. You see how guys are relaxed, they're looking in the stands, seeing who is at the game. That's sort of the typical thing for NBA players, just part of getting ready for a game. With Kobe, it was a little different; you could see that this guy is focused, ready to play. He wasn't wasting motion, he was working on things he was going to do during the game; you could see that focus. Right from the beginning of his career, I think he knew he was building up to something much bigger, that he was just at the beginning.

He was not a trash-talker from what I remember. I mean, I liked to try to get into it and try to push along the guy you're going against. Get in his head a little bit. But there are guys who are maybe more effective by not talking. In other words, they just go about their business and get their point across with a smirk or with their body language. I have seen guys try to get into Kobe's head, and he just goes down and runs a move on them, gets by them, dunks, turns and holds his chin up, and runs back down the court. Like, "Are you really trying to guard me? Does your coach really think you can guard me?" But without saying it. Michael Jordan used to talk a lot, but Kobe did it with his demeanor and his approach. The point being: Actions speak louder than words. You keep talking. I will keep dunking on you. To me, not talking can be more effective than talking a lot, for certain guys. Kobe was one of those guys.

You know, after I retired, I watched his career, like everyone. The dynamics of being on a team are so important, you learn that over the course of your career when you play. The dynamics we had in Utah with John Stockton and Karl Malone, and Jerry Sloan as the coach, everything was just perfectly in balance, the personalities there were all in balance. Karl was one way, he was out front and loud, and he did a lot of talking. John was quiet but just as tough as Karl, he would do anything he needed to do—grab, claw, push, whatever—to win the game. And Jerry Sloan was right between them; he could be quiet like John sometimes, and loud and tough like Karl at other times. When I watched what was happening with those Lakers teams early on, when they were winning championships with Shaq and Kobe and Phil Jackson, it was clear that they were out of balance. As great a coach as Phil Jackson was, even he could not bring that team into the right balance after they won a few (championships).

But still, having seen Kobe as a young guy, it was a lot of fun to watch what he became. He was so skinny when he first came in, but he really just found a way to make himself into a different player by adding muscle and taking care of his body. He always had that confidence in himself, though; that was from the beginning.

Jamal Crawford
Guard

Regular Season	Games	Wins	Losses	Win %	Field Goal %	PPG	Points (High)	RPG	APG	SPG
Bryant	28	16	12	0.57	0.463	27.1	42 (11/16/05)	5.5	5.1	2
Crawford	28	12	16	0.43	0.403	15.7	31 (12/23/07)	2.4	3.8	0.8

Résumé: *Crawford is working on his 17ᵗʰ NBA season, and he has shown only marginal signs of slowing down. He has had a career* *scoring average of 15.5 points per game, most of which have come off the bench. Crawford has played in 1,100 games, but only 432 have been starts, and Crawford has won the Sixth man of the Year three times in his career.*

Kobe connection: *Crawford is likely wrapping up his NBA career with his current stint on the Clippers, and he has been a key player in their rise in L.A., which happened to coincide with the decline and fall of the Laker empire. Crawford's teams have faced the Lakers in 28 games, and Bryant is 16-12 in those games, but it is an early loss to an otherwise-terrible Chicago team at the United Center that serves as Crawford's first memory of playing against Kobe.*

TO ME, HE has gone past being a legend. Somewhere along the line here, he has gotten to where he is not just a legend as a player, he is an icon—not just in Los Angeles, not just in this country, but globally. Everybody knows Kobe. He is the best player I ever faced. I am not saying he is Michael Jordan, because I know there is only one Michael Jordan, but for our generation he's our Michael Jordan. He had the talent and the work ethic, how driven he is, his scoring ability, his size, his athleticism, his championships, everything. I believe he is as close as you can get to Michael Jordan. And I don't think there is a player who everyone knows the way they know Kobe. It was Michael Jordan first, then Kobe Bryant came in, and did a lot of those same things, in terms of his style and his popularity.

I remember when I was in Chicago, we were just rebuilding and had a bunch of young guys, but I remember beating Kobe and those Lakers way back then; it was one of my first really good games in the NBA. It was the Kobe-Shaq Lakers, and we won. We were not going anywhere at the time, and just to beat the Lakers with Kobe and Shaq and Phil and those guys, it was cool. I think I had 24 and 10, I made some threes, it was probably my best night of that (2002-'03) season. I had some good games after that, at the end of the season, but that game helped me break through a little. I have a throwback video of that game, even now. Kobe had 36 in that game, I think, but we just played really well as a young team, and the crowd was behind us at the United Center. I don't think anyone thought we could beat the defending-champ Lakers. I think we won 30 games that year. I won't forget that one.

You have to respect how hard he works. I like Kobe, but I think even if you are someone who does not like him, you have to recognize the amount of time and dedication he puts into the game, and the fact that he doesn't shortchange himself in terms of that. I did hear that he will find a shot that, if he does not think it is going right for him, he will go to practice and just work on that shot for a half an hour. Or he will work on one move for an entire session. Just something simple that most guys don't even think to work on. He has talent, obviously, but the reason he is where he is, that's because of the work he puts in. When you put in that amount of work, it becomes automatic. He has all his moves, he has all his countermoves, and he knows them all and trusts them all because he worked hard to develop them and make sure he can have that trust in them.

I don't think there is any question that he is the toughest player I faced in my career to guard. With Kobe, whenever you are that good, that talented, there is really no stopping him. He has a certain level of freedom on the court, freedom that he has earned over his career, and that makes it tougher, because he can do things outside the offense, he can find different ways to attack. That also makes him unpredictable. He can set you up and you might not know what he is going to do. He can be unstoppable when he is like that. I remember guarding him when I was younger, and I really think my whole goal was just to not get embarrassed. I was trying to make it as tough as possible, and you can do that and hope that he misses, but he is going to score. So you just hope that you don't get embarrassed while he is scoring—hope that you don't fall, or that he does not dunk on you. If you can stay on your feet and make it tough for him, that is great. If he misses, that is even better.

A lot of people have said we won't see another Michael Jordan, and that is true. But I think we won't see another Kobe Bryant, either.

Reggie Miller
Hall of Fame guard

Regular Season	Games	Wins	Losses	Win %	Field Goal %	PPG	Points (High)	RPG	APG	SPG
Bryant	15	10	5	0.66	0.428	22.2	37 (twice)	4.8	3.7	1.5
Miller	15	5	10	0.33	0.437	19.1	39 (3/18/05)	2.9	2.3	0.9

Playoffs	Games	Wins	Losses	Win %	Field Goal %	PPG	Points (High)	RPG	APG	SPG
Bryant	5	4	1	0.80	0.367	15.6	28 (6/14/00)	4.6	4.2	1
Miller	5	1	4	0.2	0.39	22.6	35 (6/14/00)	2.8	4	0.8

Résumé: *Miller, now a broadcaster for TNT, played 18 seasons in the NBA, all with the Indiana Pacers, earning five All-Star spots and pioneering the use of the three-point shot. Miller finished his career with 2,560 three-pointers made, a league record later surpassed by Ray Allen. He twice led the league in three-pointers made and finished his career with a three-point shooting percentage of 39.5. Miller is at the top of nearly every list in the Pacers' record book, including points, minutes, games, assists, and steals. His number, 31, was retired by the Pacers, and he was inducted into the Basketball Hall of Fame in 2012.*

Kobe connection: *Miller's career mirrors some aspects of Bryant's, notably that Kobe, with 20 seasons in Los Angeles, holds the record for most consecutive seasons with one team, ahead of Tim Duncan and John Stockton (19 each), and Miller with 18 in Indiana. Like Miller, Bryant also relished the role of villain and clutch-shot maker. The two squared off in the 2000 NBA Finals, their only postseason meeting, which the Lakers won. That represented the only appearance in a Finals by Miller, who averaged 24.3 points per game in the series. Shaquille O'Neal, with 38.0 points per game and 16.7 rebounds, was the series MVP, but Bryant's* *performance in the Lakers' Game 4 win, coming back from an ankle injury and with O'Neal mired in foul trouble, saved the series for the Lakers.*

PEOPLE NEED TO understand that in 2000, when my beloved Pacers went against the Lakers, it was young Kobe that we were going against. And our focus—we knew we had to stop their entire team, obviously—but our main focus was stopping that monster in the middle by the name of Shaquille O'Neal. So the Lakers won those first two games in Staples Center and we go back to Indiana down, 2-0, but Kobe twists his ankle, I believe, in Game 2—he doesn't play in Game 3, we win in Game 3. Now, he comes back in Game 4. I don't think anyone believed he was going to come back that quickly. But he comes back, and we get Shaq in foul trouble and we think we have the game where we want it. That was the game we needed to tie the series up. We foul Shaq up, and Kobe Bryant just took over. He was unbelievable. That was part of his legacy, that was part of what made him what he is.

I love him, I hate him, and I respect him. I love him because, when you come in at 18 and you play 20 years at the shooting guard position, and to end it all with championship rings for all the fingers and one for the thumb, and you consider the amount of minutes he played, the points and the mileage that he's put on his body, that shows me a love for the game. I hate him because, in 2000 when we battled for a championship, he was just too good. Obviously, along with Shaq, that Laker team denied me the ultimate goal of winning a championship. And I respect him for what he (did at the end of his career), because you've got to take a back seat. Father Time catches up to all of us, and to have to be able to pass the torch and the legacy to the young guys on that Lakers team, like D'Angelo Russell and Julius Randle. It's tough for superstars to give an inch, and Kobe has had to take a step back and assess what's important to him. So I respect him giving back to these young guys and teaching them what it's going to take to be successful in this league.

But all of that, we saw culminated in that last game he had with the Lakers that night at Staples Center, 60 points. That desire, that hustle, that heart. But it was on full display when he was going against us in that series, especially in Game 4. You could see in his eyes what was getting ready to develop. You could see it when he looked at his bench or when he looked at his defender; he knew what he wanted to do. It was just a wonderful performance. I swear I don't know how he did not wake up the next day on life support. Just watching that game, I had to call my massage therapist just watching him take 50 shots. The next day, I was really thinking, I hope he is OK; someone needs to go check on him. If you are a Lakers fan, that one performance made everything worthwhile. The last two seasons they struggled, that one night made it all worth it. I played late into my career, but there is no way, speaking for myself, there is no way I could go into a gym by myself and put up 50 shots and score 60 points. It was an unbelievable performance.

He is, to me, the third-greatest guard to ever play the game, behind Magic and Michael Jordan. I am still in shock, still in awe of that game. You can tell what made him great, watching that game, being able to will himself to that type of performance, your last game ever, to empty all the chambers, leaving no stone unturned. It was an unbelievable performance. It goes to show you, basketball, you can see something different every day. I was just glad I got to see that one. It was an unbelievable way to go out.

Jalen Rose
Guard/forward

Regular Season	Games	Wins	Losses	Win %	Field Goal %	PPG	Points (High)	RPG	APG	SPG
Bryant	16	10	6	0.625	0.489	28	81 (1/22/06)	4.8	4.4	1.7
Rose	16	6	10	0.375	0.393	12.4	27 (3/11/03)	3.2	2.8	0.7

Playoffs	Games	Wins	Losses	Win %	Field Goal %	PPG	Points (High)	RPG	APG	SPG
Bryant	6	4	2	0.66	0.369	15.5	28 (6/14/00)	4.5	4.3	1
Rose	6	2	4	0.33	0.452	19.8	32 (6/16/00)	3.7	3	0.7

Résumé: *Rose, now an analyst for ESPN, played 13 seasons in the NBA, chosen by the Denver Nuggets with the 13ᵗʰ pick in the 1994 draft after three years at Michigan with the so-called Fab*

Five Wolverines recruiting class. Rose moved to Indiana in a trade two years into his career, and with the Pacers his career took off when he averaged 18.2 points, 4.8 rebounds, and 4.0 assists in 1999-2000. Rose helped the Pacers to the NBA Finals that year, putting up 20.8 points per game in the playoffs, but Indiana ultimately fell to the Lakers in six games. Rose was traded to Chicago two years later and closed out his career with a two-year stint in Toronto before moving to the Knicks and, finally, the Suns.

Kobe connection: *Rose played against Bryant in 16 regular-season games, during which Kobe averaged 28.0 points and shot 48.9 percent from the field. He also had five NBA Finals games against Bryant, who averaged only 15.5 points in that series to 19.8 points for Rose. That was mostly because Kobe hurt his ankle during Game 2, when he landed on Rose's foot while taking a mid-range jump shot, sending Bryant writhing to the floor in pain, clutching his left ankle. Kobe has since explained that trainer Gary Vitti popped the ankle back into place, but he did miss Game 3 of the series, a Pacers win. Rose essentially admits that he was hoping to give Bryant a twisted ankle in that series, and he'd hoped that Kobe would miss more time. Bryant got his revenge, though, when Rose was in Toronto: Rose was among the many Raptors defenders unable to quell Kobe's 81-point outburst in January 2006.*

RECALL THE FINALS that year (2000), and the playoffs before that, as being Kobe's true coming-out party.

Unfortunately for our Pacers team, we saw the passing of the baton starting in 1998, losing in the Eastern Conference finals to Michael Jordan, who went on to make the shot versus Utah that won the Finals; then he left Chicago after that year. And the next dynasty goes—where?—to Los Angeles, with the birth of Kobe Bryant, and two years later we lose to *them* in the NBA Finals. And while Shaq was the MVP in the league and was the MVP of that series, Kobe was the closer. He was the finisher. He was the Mariano Rivera. That championship helped validate him after the air balls he shot against Utah (in the 1997 playoffs). That validated that he was ready for those big moments, even the big moment with Shaq in foul trouble. That was Game 4, I believe. Shaq had foul trouble, and fouled out of that game, and Kobe was still dealing with the ankle problem. But he still managed to get 28 points, was able to get to the foul line, and, thus, there he was doing the memorable crossover dribble, making the jump shot from the top of the floor. And I just remember him, looking over at the Lakers bench with Shaq in foul trouble, and everybody maybe a little worried. It was like, "Calm down, I got this, I got this."

Kobe did get hurt in that series, while I was guarding him. I'm not proud, or I don't think it's cute or cool to say, but he didn't just accidentally hurt his ankle. I kind of played a part in that by sticking my foot in there. I think the narrative would still have been great if Kobe had retired (without that 2000 championship), and with Kobe doing so with four rings instead of the five he wound up winning. And I have one. I just wanted one. I think that's fair. But I didn't want him to get seriously injured. I just wanted him to miss a couple of games. But he did come back, and he and (Lakers trainer) Gary Vitti tell a great story about how he popped his ankle back in place after it was hurt, and rather than missing the whole series, he just missed a game. I can tell you it is a good story, because after seeing it, I didn't think that he would play. But it really just was, you know, the maturation and the birth of what became the Black Mamba.

I think that series, we would have had a chance, but they played much better from the beginning of it, and we were kind of back on our heels after the first two games in Los Angeles. They had the dramatic win in the Western Conference finals over Portland, so they were just more ready for that stage than we were.

After that, there was the 81-point game in Los Angeles. And the greatest thing about Kobe's 81-point game is that it actually wasn't his best game—not to me. His best game was actually against a good team, the Dallas Mavs, when I think he had like 60 in three quarters (62, actually, outscoring Dallas by himself, 62-61, through three quarters). We were not that good of a team at that point in Toronto.

But when I talk to people about that game, the first thing that comes to mind, I always talk about the fact that when you watch that game, Kobe never bumped his chest. He never pointed in the crowd. He never trash-talked. He was in such a zone, it was like a man amongst boys, and he literally put the smackdown on us, but he did not show any emotion in doing it. Because when you behave like that, like you want to show everyone up, like (wide receiver) Odell Beckham when he scores—really great player—but if Kobe had behaved like that, he wouldn't have got to 51, let alone 81, because we would have wanted to physically harm him on the court. But he just was very steady, and just took over. That's the true respect I have for Kobe Bryant, that he's such a tireless worker as an all-time great player. In moments like that, when he's just in the zone, his discipline and focus is unmatched in a lot of ways. That's why he had the career he has had. I always laughed when people said he did not pass enough. If you could score 81 points in an NBA game, why would you ever want to pass?

Richard Jefferson
Forward

Regular Season	Games	Wins	Losses	Win %	Field Goal %	PPG	Points (High)	RPG	APG	SPG
Bryant	24	12	12	0.50	0.394	23.2	46 (11/27/05)	5.3	6.1	1
Jefferson	24	12	12	0.50	0.443	12.3	29 (4/1/09)	4.3	1.8	0.7

Playoffs	Games	Wins	Losses	Win %	Field Goal %	PPG	Points (High)	RPG	APG	SPG
Bryant	4	4	0	1.00	0.514	26.8	36 (6/9/02)	5.8	5.3	1.5
Jefferson	4	0	4	0	0.524	6.8	10 (6/7/02)	4.5	1.3	1.0

Résumé: Jefferson has spent 15 seasons in the NBA, establishing himself as a solid scorer and all-around producer in the early part of his career, when he averaged 18.9 points and 5.7 rebounds over six seasons with the New Jersey Nets, from 2002 to 2008. He bounced around to six different teams after leaving the Nets, going from Milwaukee to San Antonio to Golden State, Utah, Dallas, and Cleveland, where he was a contributing member of the Cavaliers' 2016 NBA champions.

Kobe connection: *Jefferson's first season in the NBA featured a surprise trip by the Nets to the Finals, where he was coming off the bench behind Keith Van Horn. But because he was much more engaged defensively than Van Horn, coach Byron Scott made sure Jefferson wound up playing significant minutes. The problem for Jefferson and all of the Nets, though, was that their opponent was the Lakers, and L.A. had just come off a grueling series against the Sacramento Kings in the West finals. The Lakers, starring Kobe Bryant (26.8 points per game in the series, plus 5.8 rebounds and 5.3 assists) and Shaquille O'Neal, steamrolled the Nets in four games. In general, though, Jefferson has fared well in 24 games against Bryant—both players' teams won 12 games each.*

IT WAS GREAT to be in the NBA Finals at the back end of my career, because, really, my first memories of being in the NBA Finals were not as good, when I was with the Nets. When I was a rookie, we went in and played the Lakers, and we thought we had a chance to stay with them and win. But it was Shaq on the inside and Kobe on the perimeter, and it was too much. You know, I grew up in L.A. and I was a fan of Magic Johnson and those teams, but going back to L.A. to try to play that team, they were too much. The year before, I was at Arizona and we went to the national championship game and lost, so I remember telling myself we had to win the NBA championship because I did not want to lose two in a row. But we lost to the Lakers and we lost the next year, too. I wound up losing to Argentina in the Olympics. I did not want to lose anymore. You don't realize how hard it is just to get there when you are that young. I was lucky to be able to get back.

Back at that time, Kobe was a great player, but Shaq was the one who was in the middle; he was the nucleus of that team. He was at his peak, and we did not have anyone who could stop him. But Kobe was such a great one-on-one player that when Shaq was out or if we did a good job keeping it away from Shaq, Kobe was going to be able to create something. He had just really come into his own. We had a lot of trouble with Shaq in that series, but I just remember that even when we were able to have some success against Shaq, keep the ball out of his hands or get him in foul trouble, Kobe was there, too. You know, some people said we should have double-teamed Shaq more, but then it would give an advantage of Kobe. I am not sure anything would have worked. We played zone defense a lot in the playoffs, but that was not going to help against that team.

Kobe, he did so much for the game, though. I think when you step back, you can really appreciate how much he meant to the NBA, and to the popularity of the league. Obviously, he showed he could do it without Shaq when he won championships with the Lakers after that, so he proved that to anyone who doubted him, and you really saw how great he had become. It is something that, as a player, you appreciate how hard he worked and how great his talent is. I was lucky to be able to play against him on that level, and to be able to play with LeBron James on the same level all those years later. When you get older, you appreciate things like this. I did not know how lucky I was when I was that young to be in that situation, because it is hard to get to the NBA Finals, let alone win one. And Kobe won five of them.

Chris Webber

Forward

Regular Season	Games	Wins	Losses	Win %	Field Goal %	PPG	Points (High)	RPG	APG	SPG
Bryant	24	12	12	0.50	0.459	26.2	48 (1/6/06)	7	5	1.5
Webber	24	12	12	0.50	0.441	21.3	36 (4/14/00)	10.2	4.5	1.7

Playoffs	Games	Wins	Losses	Win %	Field Goal %	PPG	Points (High)	RPG	APG	SPG
Bryant	16	11	5	0.687	0.455	29.3	48 (5/13/01)	6.4	3.9	1.3
Webber	16	5	11	0.313	0.461	24.8	34 (5/6/01)	10.9	5.4	1.1

Résumé: Webber, the No. 1 pick of the 1993 draft when he came out of Michigan, played 15 seasons in the NBA, his best years coming in Sacramento from 1998-2005, when he earned four of his five All-Star selections. Webber won the Rookie of the Year award in 1994 for the Warriors, but Golden State took the odd step of trading him in an ill-advised deal for Tom Gugliotta. In all, Webber averaged 20.7 points in his career in the league, adding 9.8 rebounds and 4.2 assists. But despite his vast array of experience in the NBA—he played for five teams—Webber was never able to advance to the Finals.

Kobe connection: *The 2002 Western Conference finals featured Webber, Kings big man Vlade Divac, and star guard Mike Bibby, but Sacramento, despite gaining a 3-2 advantage in the series, ultimately lost the next two games, allowing the Lakers to advance. In the years after, suspicions about the integrity of the series grew, including an accusation from disgraced referee Tim Donaghy that the Lakers received favored treatment in Game 6. Regardless, the Lakers won Game 6, getting 31 points from Bryant, and took Game 7 in overtime, with Kobe scoring 30 points. Over their careers, Bryant and Webber split the 24 games in which they saw each other in regular-season matchups. But in the playoffs, Kobe had a distinct advantage, winning 11 of 16 games, and scoring 29.3 points per game.*

IT WAS HARD on us, because we matched up well with those Lakers teams. I think playing us prepared them for the next series. It was something special to see Kobe battle, because you always knew he was going to be prepared. I understand that he gets compared to different athletes, having gone against him and hearing some of the same descriptions of Peyton Manning, about being prepared, and about playing, and the mental toughness it takes to play at that level. You knew he lived for the big moments, you knew he lived to take big shots and make them, you knew that you needed to be prepared.

When I think of him, I think that when they talk about great players making other players better, it is not just the players on your team. I know that players were more serious when they had to play *against* him, I know that they were more prepared when they had to play against him, and I know they knew that they had to try to bring their best against him. You saw a change in guys because they just had to raise their level. I saw guys who had nothing but funny bones in their bodies on most days, joking around and fooling around, get serious and get ready to play when he walked into the building. And when I think of him, I think of the fact that everybody knew he was going to do everything he could, he was going to prepare himself as much as he could, to play as well as he could in those big moments.

In Sacramento, in that Western Conference Finals, I got the young, high-jumping, shooting-in-your-face, not-passing Kobe. That is probably the scariest Kobe of all. We had to deal with Shaq, too, no question. But at that time, there was no Shaq without Kobe. He had come into his own by then; he could beat you as a scorer in every way you could imagine. And he would do it in a different way every time. He would run through what he wanted to do, get to a certain spot, then he would do something different than he did the time before, or the time before that. Kobe and Michael Jordan are the only guys I have ever seen who can make a jumper after making a two-dribble move. That takes a lot of practice and a lot of precision, they're the only guys I have seen do that. He also had the fadeaway mastered, so he could turn and shoot it over either shoulder. If those shots are falling, there is nothing you can do.

Most guys, you could identify three or four things they wanted to do. Kobe could do nine or ten things on any given play. Shaq, we knew what he was going to do. He was going to put his shoulder down and get to the basket. But Kobe would change it up. To get the best of Kobe with Shaq on the floor and Phil Jackson on the sideline playing puppet master—imagine that. And Phil was very good at understanding the players he had around Shaq and Kobe, and making sure he had the right guys out there to complement what those two guys could do. So, a Derek Fisher, a Rick Fox, obviously Robert Horry, the offense had them in position to score and make you pay almost as much as Kobe and Shaq.

For me personally, I didn't have the chance to actually win a championship because I played against those two great Hall of Famers (Bryant and O'Neal) and a great Hall of Fame coach. Kobe did not even hit his peak with those teams, though. After Shaq left, that is when I really saw the competitiveness. I saw him get better every year. I saw him get better and work on different things every year. It is great to celebrate the legacy of a great player on the court. It will become even clearer in the future how great a player he was. It was an honor to battle against him. One of the best ever. One of the greatest competitors ever.

Brent Barry

Guard/forward

Regular Season	Games	Wins	Losses	Win %	Field Goal %	PPG	Points (High)	RPG	APG	SPG
Bryant	35	18	17	0.514	0.42	24.6	43 (3/6/06)	5.3	3.9	1.9
Barry	35	17	18	0.486	0.468	9.3	21 (2/14/02)	2.7	4	0.9

Playoffs	Games	Wins	Losses	Win %	Field Goal %	PPG	Points (High)	RPG	APG	SPG
Bryant	8	6	2	0.75	0.505	27.3	39 (5/29/08)	5.9	3.9	1.8
Barry	8	2	6	0.25	0.475	7.3	23 (5/27/08)	1.5	1.6	0.8

Résumé: *Barry played 14 seasons in the NBA, suiting up for five franchises over the course of his career. He won the league's slam-dunk contest in 1996 while playing for the Clippers, but Barry's best years in the NBA came when he was in Seattle, including the 2002-'03 season, in which he averaged 14.4 points, 5.4 rebounds, and 5. 3 assists, and shot 50.8 percent from the field. Barry was later waived by the rebuilding Sonics and signed on in San Antonio, where he helped win two championships for the Spurs.*

Kobe connection: *Barry twice faced Bryant's Lakers in the post-season, while he was with the Spurs in 2008 and while with the Rockets in 2009; the Lakers won both meetings. But, as Barry pointed out, the teams he played for were smart enough to keep* *him from having to guard Bryant too often, leaving that task to better defensive players.*

THINK I WAS pretty lucky, the way my career was timed, just having a whole career where I was basically playing alongside Kobe Bryant. I came in just a year behind Kobe, and I have been able to be in broadcasting since then, so not only my career but to be able to sit and watch him as many years as I have, seeing him compete at a high level is remarkable. He does so many different things to beat you. He is a very difficult guy to guard, for obvious reasons. He just knows that if you're too close to him he can get by you, and if you are too far off him, he can make a jumper. He can make that read very, very quickly; he is going to expose mistakes if you make them.

During playoff time, thankfully, coaches are really smart, and they generally put the best defender on the guy who might play your position. So I was not matched up that much against Kobe at playoff time, when we saw them, the two times I played against Kobe in the postseason—at least in 2008, and the next year in Houston. But some of the regular season matchups we had, especially when I was in Seattle, those were the best years I remember. We had one year, we beat the Lakers four times (in 2001), the year they went on to win the championship with Shaq and Kobe, and when we had Gary Payton on that team, Vin Baker, Patrick Ewing. We beat them four times, but we did

75

not make the playoffs; we finished a few games out of that race in the West.

The battles Kobe had with Ray Allen up there were very memorable. They came into the league together, and they really did have a personal rivalry. They just didn't like each other very much, which was strange because Ray did not really get into that aspect of the game. But I can remember games where Kobe had 30 or more points, and Ray would have 30 or more, because they both wanted to attack each other. I just remember Kobe's focus on wanting to go through everybody. That's basically it. It was, "I'm going to win at all costs," and sometimes it might have cost him some cachet and some things with his own teammates. But it was about the drive to win. I have no problem saying that about him. He's not unlike somebody I grew up with in that way, somebody people have heard of (Barry's father, Rick Barry, who is, like Bryant, known to be a demanding character). Nowadays, there are just more ways that people accept that sort of mental approach to the game, and that will to win and desire to compete at that level. But those will be fond memories I have of Kobe, for sure. I had the ability to compete against one of the best guards ever in the game.

The interesting thing about playing my whole career against him is that (early on) you didn't know what he was going to be, and how great he was going to be. The type of impact he had on the generation of players we are watching now—what it is he did to them in their belief in their skill set, their belief in how competitive you have to be—I think that's the lasting mark of what Kobe Bryant represents to the NBA, his tenacious work ethic.

Jeff Van Gundy
Coach

Résumé: Van Gundy broke into the NBA as an assistant coach with the Knicks in 1989, working under four different head coaches before being given the head coaching job in 1996. The Knicks won a playoff spot in each of Van Gundy's years as a head coach and went to the NBA Finals in the lockout-shortened 1999-2000 season. After departing New York, Van Gundy coached for four seasons in Houston but could not get much traction with the Rockets due to frequent injuries to stars Tracy McGrady and Yao Ming. After he was let go by Houston in 2007, Van Gundy got into broadcasting with ESPN. His all-time coaching record was 430-318.

Kobe connection: Besides having broadcasted some of Bryant's big moments, Van Gundy has also seen Kobe as an opposing coach, even facing him in a 2004 playoff series that the Lakers won in five games, with Bryant averaging 24.4 points, 5.6 rebounds, and 6.2 assists.

FOR ME, I think sometimes the hardest thing to do is to end a storied career, anybody's storied career, gracefully, and I think you were able to see a different Bryant personality coming out: patient, embracing seemingly every game, and every arena, and every fan. Everywhere they went. It surprised me just because it was almost like a personality transformation when you watch after games. Before he was very stoic and focused, and he would talk about games, but that was it. And then in his last year, it was very, very endearing, really, to everyone: other players, coaches, officials. Certainly going through (that) last year without a chip on his shoulder, and because the Lakers were so bad at the end, I think it's absolutely the right personality to show in your swan song.

Think about it. He was in the NBA for half his life, almost half his life. It is an unusual way to approach things; he was always going to be in a unique place. He was 17 when he came in, and then he was leaving as an adult and a father of two, I believe. That is pretty impressive; it is such a long, long time. And to do it all with one team, and to do it with the team that is going to have you in the public eye over and over, in Los Angeles. I always respected first his greatness, but also his competitive edge. He gave himself to his profession. He had talent, but he also had a lot of competitiveness, and that drove him in the offseason, it drove his work habits. You can have talent but not be great. Kobe had talent, he had the work ethic, and he put that all together. You saw it in the results on the floor, how difficult it was for opposing players to guard him and for opposing coaches to figure out what to do about him.

Obviously, we had a lot of battles with Kobe in Houston; we had a playoff series against them. More than anything, when you are going against him as a player or a coach, as much as you want to stop him, you have to respect his talent and his greatness, just the level that he can compete at. But you take that, and I think what I always respected even more about him is the way he had such a love of the game. All he wanted to do was compete, and he was going to put everything he had into it. He sacrificed so much, he put everything he had into the game, and that is not an easy thing to do for 20 years the way he did it. He had talent, yes, but you could see it was the work habits that made him what he was.

Brian Shaw
Guard

Regular Season	Games	Wins	Losses	Win %	Field Goal %	PPG	Points (High)	RPG	APG	SPG
Bryant	3	1	2	0.33	0.538	17.7	25 (11/9/97)	3.7	4.3	1.3
Shaw	3	2	1	0.66	0.364	5.7	8 (3/23/97)	1.7	4	1.7

Résumé: *Shaw spent 14 seasons in the NBA, playing for six differ-ent teams before landing with the Lakers in 1999, when he was 33 years old. Shaw had his best seasons in Boston when he was drafted out of UC Santa Barbara, and though a contract dispute sent him to play in Italy for a year in 1989-'90, he returned to average 13.8 points per game and 7.6 assists for the Celtics in 1990-'91. For all his time in the NBA, though, Shaw will be best remembered for* *his contributions as an aging combo guard off the bench at the end of his career with the Lakers, where he not only provided valuable mistake-free backup minutes, but also acted as a veteran influence in a tumultuous locker room.*

Kobe connection: *Shaw has known Bryant since he skipped the NBA to play in Italy for a year and met his father, Joe Bryant. He was part of the Lakers from 1999 to 2003, frequently quelling some of the fires that erupted between Bryant and O'Neal. Shaw then joined the team's coaching staff from 2005 to 2011 and had Kobe's blessing to take over the job when Phil Jackson retired. The Lakers went with Mike Brown, though, and Shaw moved on, eventually becoming head coach of the Nuggets from 2013 to 2015. After he was fired from that job, Shaw returned to L.A. and was an assistant coach with the Lakers during Bryant's final season.*

I **KNEW KOBE WHEN** he was a kid and I was playing in Italy; I knew his father. Then when I came back and I was in Orlando, his dad brought him to one of our games with the Magic, and I could not believe how much he had grown. I think he was a junior in high school, and I was 6-6 and he was my size already. The last time I had seen him, you know, he was just a kid, but now he is walking around like a grown man. I remember he said to me that in a year he was going to be in the NBA playing against me. And I did not really know what he meant; I thought maybe he had the years wrong or something, because he was going to have to go to college for a couple of years. But he knew he was going to make it in the NBA. So I mean, an encounter like that, it kind of sticks with you, and then when I heard how good he had gotten and he winds up getting drafted, there he is playing for the Lakers. Give him credit, he was right.

Winning the championships with those teams, that was definitely the highlight. But everything else that was going on was difficult, to have everything go back and forth in public, in the media, and sort of leave it for the rest of us to clean up, people asking all of us whose side we were on. The thing was, when they stopped talking and just played, just focused on the game, they still could mostly put all of that stuff aside and win. I thought that winning would cover all that up, but I guess the organization disagreed; they thought it was enough. It was hard to wrap your mind around, though, as good as those teams were.

For Kobe, that was tough. But, everything that he went through, I can't have anything but respect for his career and what a legend he became, because he had a real toughness. It was something that I saw day in and day out: his willingness to compete, his desire to beat you at no matter what it was you were doing. In practice he was that way. He would go at his own teammates in practice. It didn't matter, he wanted to win. He was always going to compete at a high level, and try to play his game and will the rest of the team to lift up its level. I think in the last couple of years he had a harder time with that, because he had so many injuries, and it seemed like the injuries just kept coming and coming and there was nothing he could do. I think because of the team being the way it was, he might have liked to be more of a passer, more of a facilitator, but the team just had a lot of young players who were learning. Kobe really does not get credit for how good of a passer he is, but he does not have a lot of patience when he's trying to facilitate and the guys he is passing to aren't hitting shots.

(The last year), it was good that he let up a little bit. He would still have some times when he looked like his old self, and that is when you know he is going to be dangerous. Because it is all up in his head, he has all that stored. Every day I played with him, I saw it pretty much every day. He would take time and just run through some fundamentals, just run through some things in terms of his footwork, you know, 20 minutes or a half hour. And he would do it every day, things you might have done in high school. But he kept his footwork fresh by doing that, he kept it all at the front of his head. So if he is able to get by you and get to his spot, he is going to know exactly what he wants to do, he has been running it through his head and practicing it every day for 20-something years.

That does include the clutch situations. He is, to me, the best in the history of the game when it comes to that. Him and Michael Jordan, and you would have to give Jordan an advantage because he has six championships, Kobe has got five. But I don't think you could say that Michael has more killer instinct than Kobe. I think they're right on the same level as far as that goes. I have seen Kobe do it more, personally, so I just know how he is when the situation is close: the game slows down for him. It speeds up for a lot of guys. It always slowed down for him; that is something that made him different, that made him great.

I think the thing that will stand out to me really is how, when he hurt his Achilles, you're not supposed to walk on that. I think a lot of guys, they're getting carried off the floor if they have that injury. Kobe knew how bad it was, but he could handle the pain. He has a tolerance for pain, a high tolerance. That says a lot about him.

PART 3:

A LAKER REBIRTH

"**W**ITH KOBE, HE was so good, you could throw all the analytics out the window, you could forget trying to play against his tendencies and all of that. You had to give him looks, he was going to get his looks. And then you just had to hope he would miss." –*Grant Hill*

THE LAKERS, SO close to a dynasty that could have exceeded what Phil Jackson's Bulls accomplished, were set aflame and doomed to an eventual breakup. Perhaps the one thing that could have saved the team might have been a 2004 championship, which they were heavily favored to win after winning 56 games and surviving the Spurs and Timberwolves in the West playoffs. But the Pistons—a team-oriented group that did not rely on any one superstar and were portrayed in the media as the anti-Lakers—stifled the Lakers with their defense, holding Bryant to just 38.1 percent shooting, while Malone's knee problem forced him to miss a game in the series and limited him when he did play. Payton, too, was ineffective, and Detroit was able to expose the Lakers' lack of depth.

When it was over, the Lakers knew they had to act. The Shaq-Kobe feud had grown too heated, and the team had run its course. In July 2004, facing an ultimatum from Bryant—who said he would leave the following summer in free agency if O'Neal was on the team—the Lakers traded O'Neal to Miami. And the changes did not stop there: Bryant signed an extension immediately after the O'Neal deal, Jackson stepped down as coach a few weeks before it, and the Lakers made the ill-fated hire of Rudy Tomjanovich, who would pull out of the job just 43 games into his tenure. Spurs coach Gregg Popovich said after the departure of O'Neal, "I hated it, personally.... I'd rather have him there and have the Lakers be the Lakers, to be honest. The competitive part of me feels like the Soviet Union just disbanded. You don't know who to go after. Obviously there are enough good teams, but the rest of us are all sort of equal. The Lakers were the Lakers. When you win three in a row, you get to have the status. And I hate the fact that they're gone."

They were not, however, gone for too long. The Lakers caught the first of two major breaks after that difficult 2004-'05 season, though. Jackson agreed to return as coach, despite the fact that the Lakers had Bryant and very little else to work with. But Jackson managed to withstand a weak roster—the hapless Smush Parker and the much-besmirched Kwame Brown were starters for the Lakers—to earn consecutive play-off berths.

But Bryant's frustration with the roster built—even after a historic performance in the winter of 2006, when he laid 81 points on the Toronto Raptors—and despite public pleas for a trade in the summer of 2007, the Lakers held onto Bryant, hoping instead to make a deal of their own that would catapult them back into contention. On February 1, 2008, the Lakers finally were able to find their man, trading for Grizzlies star forward Pau Gasol. Bryant immediately approved, saying, "It shows a great deal of commitment from the organization. It's a matter of us gelling now and putting it together."

The Lakers did. They went 29-9 to close out the year, and Gasol meshed easily with the team, averaging 18.8 points and

7.8 rebounds, shooting 58.9 percent from the field. In the Western Conference playoffs, the Lakers rolled, losing just three games against their 12 wins. The Lakers were contenders once again and would face the franchise's oldest rival, the Celtics, in two out of three NBA Finals from 2008-'10.

Rick Barry
Hall of Fame forward

Résumé: *Barry was one of the biggest stars of the late 1960s and '70s, spending 14 years in the ABA and NBA, earning 12 All-Star spots, and averaging 24.8 points per game. He was the NBA's Rookie of the Year in 1966 and led the NBA in scoring in 1966-67 while he was with the San Francisco Warriors, with an average of 35.6 points. Barry put forth one of the greatest performances in the history of the NBA Finals when he helped power the Warriors to a sweep of the heavily favored Washington Bullets in 1975. Barry was MVP of the series and averaged 29.5 points, 4.0 rebounds, and 5.0 assists in the four games. He was inducted into the Basketball Hall of Fame in 1987. He was voted one of the NBA's 50 Greatest Players as part of the NBA's 50th anniversary project in 1996.*

Kobe connection: *Barry has been a longtime friend of Bryant's, sharing Kobe's reputation of being too demanding and brusque with less-talented teammates, and being generally disliked by opposing players during their younger days. In part because of that, Barry has been a frequent defender of Bryant. In 2009, he told a radio host who was criticizing Kobe, "You don't like Kobe and there's a lot of people who don't like Kobe, but hey, you're entitled to your opinion, and that's great. Good for you. But the thing about it is, don't sit here and try to tell me about it, about Kobe is this, because I don't agree with you."*

I HAVE KNOWN KOBE for a long time, obviously. What I respect about Kobe as a player of his stature is that he showed up every night he put his uniform on, and he gave you everything he had. I think it was ingrained in him, and I don't think every player, even the best ones, does it every time. With him, you could just tell, he is a competitor—he wanted to win and he wanted to do his best. He was maligned at times, unjustifiably, and I always thought that was unfair. I was always a big Kobe fan, and it always bothered me that some people did not recognize the sacrifices he made and how special it was, the level of effort he put out every time. I love the way he competes. I think he was maligned because of his success, and maybe because he did not "play the game" with teammates and the media as much as other people did. It would always irritate me when I heard people talk about him that way, that he could only win with (Lakers teammate Shaquille O'Neal). I think he proved all of those people wrong.

He was called selfish, which is absurd. He was on a team for a while there that, if he did not try to do everything he tried to do, would have no chance at winning. When they got some players in there who were good at doing it, who could support him, they won. I was happy for him when he won championships after Shaq left, because everybody said he couldn't do it. Well, he did it. He got Pau Gasol, they had Lamar Odom, they got all those guys together and they won. Before that, he wanted so badly to win that he went out and took a lot of shots; he tried so hard to do everything. Here's the thing: if you have got teammates and somebody's open, but you can get the shot off and the guy who is open is not as good a shooter as you, why the hell would you throw it to him? That's not good basketball. Everybody would tell him to pass more, make the extra pass. Well, bullshit. The extra pass doesn't mean anything if the guy can't shoot. The shot with the hand in your face, if you are Kobe Bryant, might be a better percentage shot than anything you're going to get from a teammate who is wide open but can't shoot.

People are always trying to knock someone off the pedestal. People are jealous of other people's success, so it is almost as though the more success you have, the more intensely people are going to look for flaws and find shortcomings. That happened with Kobe on the Lakers as much as anyone in the league, really. You didn't see people trying to find flaws with Derek Fisher or Rick Fox. But nobody's perfect. It happens, it comes with the territory, and you have to learn to accept it. The whole thing is, you have to learn to be tone-deaf to that stuff. You personally have to learn to have great pride in what you do, and as long as you know that you're doing things the right way and giving your best effort, what other people think should not influence you. Does it hurt at times? Yeah. But as long as you know the truth. I had to go through that bullshit, people expressing opinions about me, people writing things about me who have never even met me, saying things about me even though they never spent any time with me. There's a lot of hearsay and things like that. And I watched Kobe go through it.

I am not saying it's not hurtful, but the thing is, you have got to let it roll off your back. It is part of maturing. I used to think, when I was in my 20s, that I was mature, and people might say I was immature, and I would say, "No, I'm not, what are you talking about?" But then you get into your 30s and you realize how immature you really were. That's when you let things roll off your back, that is a point Kobe reached. Because as long as you know who you are and your friends and family know who you are, the other stuff people say doesn't matter. Kobe learned that, and I've always been a big Kobe supporter because of it. If everybody in the NBA who put on a uniform gave the effort that Kobe gave, the league would be much better off.

I have always felt that if you went back and looked, if someone studied all the film, certainly in the games I saw, Shaq got more assists from Kobe Bryant than anybody else in his time with the Lakers. He was a better passer than anyone else on those teams. And I always think, somewhere down the road, both Shaq and Kobe are going to hit themselves on the head and say, "What the hell were we thinking?" They had a chance to do something so incredibly special that they would have been talking about those Lakers the way they talk about the Boston Celtics in the era that they had with Bill Russell and Bob Cousy in the 1960s. But because of petty little meaningless things, they gave up that opportunity. They could have won a whole bunch of championships with the way that they were, as good as those two were at the time. They could have been an unbelievable juggernaut for a number of years.

I don't think he was a selfish player. He was a creator, he created shots. He was a heck of an athlete. He could go to the basket, he could make his free throws, he could shoot it. He was a scorer and a shooter. He was both. And there's a difference. A scorer finds multiple ways to put points on the board. A shooter just shoots. Kobe could shoot, but he could find other ways to get shots, too, for his team. Scorers do it every way, on the fast break, getting to the free-throw line, driving to the basket. He was a very good defender, too, a really good and smart team defender. That was Kobe. He was multidimensional. He could do it all.

I was jealous of him that he had the chance to have a great career and do it with one team. I wonder if we will see that very much anymore. A guy like Kobe or Tim Duncan. That is going to be very rare. I was very happy with the way he was able to go out, even though the Lakers were not very good. That final game, he scores 60 points, that was pretty much the perfect ending. It was a nice tribute to a guy who gave his heart, body, and soul for the game.

Grant Hill

Forward

Regular Season	Games	Wins	Losses	Win %	Field Goal %	PPG	Points (High)	RPG	APG	SPG
Bryant	34	26	8	0.765	0.491	26.7	49 (3/1/09)	6.2	5.5	1.3
Hill	34	8	26	0.235	0.473	15.1	34 (1/18/97)	6.4	3.6	1.1

Playoffs	Games	Wins	Losses	Win %	Field Goal %	PPG	Points (High)	RPG	APG	SPG
Bryant	6	4	2	0.66	0.521	33.7	40 (5/17/10)	7.2	8.3	0.8
Hill	6	2	4	0.33	0.438	9.8	23 (5/19/10)	4.3	2.2	0.8

Résumé: Small forward Grant Hill came into the NBA with the Pistons as a star out of Duke in 1994 and would have been a certain Hall of Famer if he had not suffered a devastating ankle injury that eventually took away more than three years of his career. Still, Hill earned seven All-Star spots in his career and was named the NBA's Rookie of the year in 1995. Hill played 19 years in the NBA, averaging 16.7 points, 6.0 rebounds, and 4.1 assists, and was at his best in the 2000 season, when he averaged 25.8 points per game, third in the league. Despite his injury history, Hill retired at age 40 in 2013, while playing for the Clippers, his fourth NBA team.

Kobe connection: Hill and Bryant likely would have formed a long-standing rivalry if Hill had not gotten injured. Both came from similar backgrounds: Hill was the son of NFL great Calvin Hill, while Kobe's father, Joe Bryant, was an NBA and European League veteran and played the same position, filling up box scores not just with scoring, but with passing and rebounding, too. In *all, Hill saw Bryant in 34 regular-season games, with the Lakers winning 26 of them. The two also faced off in the 2010 Western Conference finals, which Kobe helped win for the Lakers with 37 points in the clinching Game 6.*

IT'S WEIRD; I am one of the only people who is old enough to have played pretty much with Kobe at every stage of his career. The last few years, he was hurt, I was still in the league. But I remember playing against him his rookie year, and I also remember playing against him in 2012-'13, before he tore his Achilles. So, I had experience being on the court against him at all those times. It's been really interesting.

Early on, as he was trying to establish himself on a talented Lakers team, you saw the potential. You saw what Jerry West saw before he drafted him. But I don't think you could ever envision, back in 1996, in 1997, what he would eventually become. All of a sudden, he emerged and became a star, and one of the great players. I remember battling against him when I was in Detroit. I didn't play much against him when I was in Orlando. But later on, I was being asked to guard him when I was in Phoenix. I was older then, and it was a different role for me. It was almost unfair. But it was always a challenge for sure.

I think the thing I respected about him most was, back in 1996-'97, when I was with the Pistons, we played against him and we actually beat the Lakers in a double-overtime game. It was a crazy game at the Forum. Del Harris was their coach and Kobe was not getting many minutes before that, but it was double-overtime, so they had to play him some more, and he got 30 minutes or so. But he came into the game and he got the ball pretty quickly, and it was like, he went right at you. There was no hesitation, there was no sort of sense that he was a teenage kid and a rookie who was intimidated. He scored 20-something points that night; it was one of the first times he had scored that much. (Bryant had 21 in the game, only his second 21-point game.) He was not trying to just fit in. It was like, "I'm here." That was my first initial impression. This kid has no fear.

He was coming off the bench, Eddie Jones was the 2-guard at the time. A year or two later, he was an All-Star, but at that time he was still just coming off the bench. I had played against Kevin Garnett the year before, and I remember with him he would come into the game and you could tell he was just trying to figure it all out, he had not established himself. He got there, obviously, he did figure it out. But Kobe, there was none of that. Kobe was like, "I'm here, I'm not going to be denied." He had that mindset throughout his entire career, but he came into the league with it.

In Phoenix, I was guarding him at 37, 38, and that was a challenge for sure. It was one of those things where, of all the guys I had to guard at that time, he was by far the toughest. He was relentless, he was so skilled, he was so intelligent about positioning and reach, and all of the little things. Certain guys, even All-Stars, you can guard and you have a game plan. You can figure it out and think, "If I stay with the game plan, I have a chance of making their life difficult and doing a good job."

But with Kobe, he was so good, you could throw all the analytics out the window, you could forget trying to play against his tendencies and all of that. You had to give him looks, he was going to get his looks. And then you just had to hope he would miss.

You also need a selective memory against him. Because you could do everything right. You could be on him, you could guess right on what he was going to do, you could time it perfectly, everything. And you turn around, and the ball goes in. And you go, "Well, OK." It can play with your head a little bit. With him, every possession you had to be engaged; you had to be paying attention, you had to be ready. Because he was ready.

I did remember some battles in the Detroit years. He is one of the guys who, when I look at my career and I look at the injuries and I think what could have been, he is one of the guys I think about. It would have been fun from like 2000 to 2006 to go against him. He was sort of, during that period of time, he was the gold standard. He would have been someone I would have enjoyed and looked forward to that matchup, but I never had that chance. Obviously, I regret not being healthy, but, man, to go against a guy like that, when you can be healthy and in your prime? That would have been fun. That is a matchup I would have liked to have been part of, year in and year out.

Morris Peterson

Forward

Regular Season	Games	Wins	Losses	Win %	Field Goal %	PPG	Points (High)	RPG	APG	SPG
Bryant	19	13	6	0.684	0.469	30.2	81 (1/22/06)	6.4	5.9	1.1
Peterson	19	6	13	0.316	0.414	10.5	27 (12/22/02)	2.4	1.3	0.7

Résumé: After helping Michigan State to a national championship in 2000, a season in which he was also named Big Ten Player of the Year, Peterson was drafted by the Raptors with the 21ˢᵗ pick the following June. He went on to play 11 years in the NBA and earned fan-favorite status during his seven seasons spent with the Raptors from 2000 to 2007. He averaged 10.7 points during his career, which also featured stops in New Orleans and Oklahoma City, but it was his time in Toronto that most defined his NBA tenure. He had his most productive year in 2005-'06, when he played all 82 games and averaged 16.8 points, but unfortunately for Peterson it would be one game and one opposing player who defined that year's Raptors team.

Kobe connection: Bryant, generally speaking, liked to see Peterson's teams. In 19 matchups over their careers, Kobe averaged 30.2 points, made 46.9 percent of his shots from the field, and 43.0 percent of his three-pointers. In eight of those 19 games, Bryant scored better than 30 points, but, of course, it is the one meeting in January 2006 that has been immortalized—the night Kobe scored 81 points against the Raptors in Los Angeles. Peterson points out that, only weeks before, on December 7, Bryant had been held down by the Raptors to only 11 points, and Peterson himself (14 points) outscored him. But that game has been lost to the dustbin of history. It's forever the 81-point game that links that year's Raptors to Bryant's legacy.

HONESTLY, IT WAS a tough game. That is not the kind of history you want to be part of. But a couple of things about it that I remember: First, we had actually played him pretty well the first time we played them that season. He scored something like 11 points against us on our floor in Toronto, so we did a better job on him that game, but we lost and it was Lamar Odom and some of their other guys who beat us in that one, even though we held Kobe down. So when we played them the second time, we did not want the other guys to beat us again. But, you know, 11 points one game, 81 the other, so I guess he averaged 46 points against us, right? The other thing was, we got out to a big lead early on, we were winning that game, and it did not feel like they were going to be able to get back into it. So we stuck with what got us a lead in the first place; we didn't go after him or double-team him.

He is obviously one of the greatest players to ever play the game. He is so hard to guard. I mean, the best you're trying to do is to make him pass it. Because even if he shoots with a hand in his face, he still has a pretty good chance to make it. You make it a little tougher for him to see the rim, but he is still going to make it if he is in that rhythm. He had other games against us, other great games. My rookie year, the first time I ever faced him, he scored 40 points; that was when they had Shaq. He had 48, I think it was, one game against us (in 2004). We had some games where we locked him up, but you were not going to lock up Kobe Bryant too much. He just has too many weapons he can go to.

In the 81-point game, we had a pretty good lead in the second half, but he took over. I don't think he thought his teammates were going to help him much that game. There was a play in the second half where he threw a pass and it went straight out of bounds, because I think Lamar Odom was not looking for it. So he just shrugged and got a look in his eye, like, "I am going to have to shoot it every time." He took over from there. He was really unstoppable. You know, you just tip your cap to him. It was a great performance. Maybe we should have changed our defense, but there are a lot of guys who could not score 81 points if you did not guard them at all. Give him credit. He is a Hall of Famer, one of the greatest ever.

Chuck Swirsky
Broadcaster

Résumé: Swirsky has been involved in sports broadcasting for nearly four decades, providing play-by-play for the University of Michigan's basketball and football teams before joining the Toronto Raptors as their radio play-by-play man in 1998. He then moved to television, teaming with Canadian star Leo Rautins. Swirsky moved on to the hometown Bulls, taking over their radio play-by-play in 2008.

Kobe connection: Swirsky was in the radio booth on January 22, 2006, when the Raptors traveled to the Staples Center in Los Angeles for a mostly meaningless game. Toronto was 14-26 entering the night, after all, and the Lakers were just two games over .500, at 21-19. The night, as Swirsky and everyone else in attendance would soon learn, wound up being particularly significant in the lore of Kobe Bryant.

IT WAS A Sunday night, and it was a very pedestrian type of environment. It was a snoozefest, let's be honest. No one was there. There were no A-listers there, there were not the beautiful people of Los Angeles there. It was after the holidays, before the All-Star game, and there was not a lot of buzz. Andy Dick, who was a comedian and I guess an actor, too: he was probably the only person of celebrity status attending the game, so there was not really a whole lot of excitement about the game. It was Sunday, so that hurt, as well. You had the NFL playoff games that day, the conference championships. Our game was not a big priority.

The Lakers were going through the motions to start the game. They were sleepwalking, and their talent and skill level was not very good that year. Other than Kobe, they had Lamar Odom and, I think, Kwame Brown, Chris Mihm, players of that caliber. They really did not look like a team that wanted to be there very much, when they were down by, I believe it was, 18 points. The Raptors had a huge lead all through the first half, a huge lead even into the third quarter. The Lakers were playing almost no defense at all. Kobe was involved, he was engaged, but he was probably the only player on the Lakers who showed any spirit of competitiveness whatsoever.

He missed a couple of shots to start the second half, but then he made something like five in a row, and he was hot from the three-point line, which was not usual for him. Obviously, he got into a rhythm, and around the middle of the third quarter, as the Lakers started getting back into the ball game, he really turned it on. You could tell that he almost sensed he could bring his team back into the game by himself. There was a point when it was obvious he decided he was going to have to win the game on his own. For whatever reason, the Raptors did very little trapping; we really did not take the ball out of his hands. He was guarded by everyone on our team, it seemed, but always one-on-one, never in a double-team. Jose Calderon, the point guard, defended him, and Matt Bonner, the center, guarded him. Jalen Rose, Mo Peterson, Mike James—on and on and on. It was like no matter who the Raptors put in front of him, he would size them up and figure out how he was going to beat them. He was getting to the rim as much as he wanted. He took 20 free throws that night, and he was spectacular from the line (making 18 of them).

But it really was not until early in the fourth quarter, or the middle of the quarter, that the fans and the rest of us in the building started to get that sense of, "Wait, what are we watching here?" He had more than 50 points heading into the fourth quarter, and you would have expected him to get 60 or so. But he exploded (for 28 points) in the fourth. No one could stop him. That motor was running, the juices were going. It was marvelous to watch.

The Lakers had a cushion at the end of the game, but he went to the line and—you talk about pressure—he had 79 points. They were up by 16 or 18 points, and there was less than a minute to go. I do remember that he went to the line, and I thought, "This is pressure." The crowd is going bananas because they know what is going on. There is a big difference between 79 and 80. He could have left that gym in the history books with 79 points, brick both free throws, and been happy about that. But you walk out of the gym and say, "Hey I got 80, I got more than 80." That is amazing, to look up at the scoreboard and see that "80." The Lakers took him out of the game, the place went crazy, and it was just a perfect way for it to wrap up.

One of my greatest regrets is, I never got the chance to have him sign my box sheet, which I still have. It was unbelievable. After the game, the Raptors players were upset because, basically, it was a one-man wrecking crew. He simply destroyed the Raptors. I know some players were upset, because players have a lot of pride, and they respect Kobe obviously, but they don't want to see a player go off like that. Remember, a few weeks before, he had gotten 62 points against Dallas in the first three quarters, and did not play in the fourth quarter because the Lakers were so far ahead. So we all knew he was doing some special things that year. But the Lakers needed him on this night. I remember the plane ride after that game was silent. We were playing in Denver the next night, so it was a short flight, but a lot of players were upset, so the flight was as quiet a flight as I have been on.

It was surreal. To this day, it is the greatest single performance I have ever seen live in any sport. I saw Dick Bosman throw a no-hitter for Cleveland against Oakland, and I mean, how many no-hitters are pitched? I was at the ballpark watching that. I also saw the Bears beat the New England Patriots in the Super Bowl in 1986, in New Orleans. But as far as one individual having that level of impact, the way he carved up a whole team by himself, it was remarkable. When I reflect on that game, I always say to myself, "How many players can you say are so impactful that they can still score even when the entire arena knows he is going to get the rock?" There are not many. Everybody knew Kobe was going to get the rock. He still scored 81. It was one for the ages.

Stephen Curry

Guard

Regular Season	Games	Wins	Losses	Win %	Field Goal %	PPG	Points (High)	RPG	APG	SPG
Bryant	15	9	6	0.60	0.425	26.9	44 (twice)	5.6	4.2	1.6
Curry	15	6	9	0.4	0.446	22.9	47 (4/12/13)	4.9	7.3	1.5

Résumé: Curry won back-to-back MVP awards in 2015 and 2016, and won his first NBA championship in 2015. He led the league in scoring in 2015-'16 (30.5 points per game) and also shattered his own record for most three-pointers in a single season, sinking 402, up from 286 the previous year. In his first seven seasons in the NBA, Curry has averaged 22.4 points per game and shot an incredible 44.4 percent from the three-point line.

Kobe connection: *Curry might be a generation removed from Bryant's peak years, the league's torch having first been passed to LeBron James. But Curry has been around the NBA for years with his father, former NBA player Dell Curry, so there's no doubt that Curry has a full appreciation for Bryant's ability. Though Curry and Kobe came far from matching each other in their primes, Bryant has done more than hold his own in the two players' 15 individual meetings, which saw him win nine games and average 26.9 points. During the Warriors' record-setting 73-9 season in 2015-16, Kobe and the Lakers accounted for one of the Warriors' nine losses.*

MY FAVORITE MEMORY of Kobe was the 81-point game against Toronto, watching that. I have been hot before and made every shot I threw up there, and got on a little streak during a game. But to score 81 points, so much has to go right; the situation has to be just perfect for it. You've got to have a special talent, obviously, like Kobe, to do it. Just watching the game, it still doesn't make sense. When I watch it, I think, "'How did he do it? How did he do it?" Everybody asks me now if I think somebody will ever score 81 points again, or they ask if they think I could do it, and I don't even think it is possible, just the way the game is going and just how hard it is.

Think about it—81 points; he had 50-something in one half. I think about it, and I don't think it can be done now. There is a reason people are still talking about that game to this day, even ten years later, and they will keep talking about it. The consistency he had to show in that game is just unreal. He did not have a lot of weapons on that team, and Toronto did not seem to be able to figure it out. It boggles your mind. It's special. I could see getting to 50, and maybe pushing it from there to 60. But 81?

He's a legend, an accomplished legend at that. He changed the game and inspired an entire generation to go out there and try to be your best. He demanded greatness from himself and his teammates, every team he was on. He was very open about that. But he has also talked to me and given me advice. He has done that with a lot of guys around the league in the last couple of years. I think he inspired my leadership qualities more than my actual game, just the way he came out every day with that competitiveness, that fire. And he was always all about winning; that was what he wanted to do. He obviously won a lot. He has five championships, and he did that because he put the time in and did the work.

Doc Rivers
Coach

Résumé: *Rivers was a solid NBA point guard for 13 seasons, earning a spot in the 1988 All-Star game while with the Atlanta Hawks, where he played eight years. He also played for the Clippers, Knicks, and Spurs, finishing his playing days with a scoring average of 10.9 points and adding 5.7 assists per game. Rivers went right from playing to broadcasting and got into coaching soon after that, taking over the Orlando Magic at the young age of 36. He won the NBA's Coach of the Year in his first season, leading an undermanned Magic team to a 41-41 record. He was fired by the Magic after a 1-10 start in 2003 but was quickly hired by the Celtics after the season. In Boston, once the Celtics secured stars Ray Allen and Kevin Garnett to go with Paul Pierce and Rajon Rondo, Rivers led the Celtics to two NBA Finals, in 2008 and 2010.*

Kobe connection: *In those Finals, Rivers just happened to face the Celtics' oldest rival, the Lakers, who were armed not only with Bryant, but with big men Pau Gasol and Lamar Odom. Rivers and his Celtics were able to stave off the Lakers in 2008, finishing the series with an emphatic, 39-point Game 6 win. Kobe returned the favor in 2010, however, leading the Lakers to a tense, thrilling seven-game Finals win over the Celtics.*

THE 2008 YEAR, I remember that. The 2010 year, I try not to remember too much. But in those Finals, I just remember how hard Kobe was to deal with every night, the number of things he was able to do. It's tough. He is, physically, a great player. Obviously, everybody knows that. But in both of those series, it was the mental part of Kobe that stood out to me, more than the talent. I don't think you really know a player—because we see guys for a game, then we move on to the next game—I don't think you know a guy until you have either coached him or coached against him in the playoffs, and seen what he does in terms of his habits and how he thinks. Kobe is very smart. He is like a lot of great players; he is a basketball savant. He knows the game on a very personal level, and it's really neat.

The 2008 Finals, Game 6 was terrific. That's a moment that I remember in 2008. The funniest moment to me, and Kobe knows this, the funniest moment of the thing was when we were up by something like 1,000 points in Game 6 and the guy who you would least expect walks over to me during the game, Tom Thibodeau (who was then a Celtics assistant coach). And he asks me, "Are you going to sub out? There's six minutes and we're up 42 points." Of all the guys to say that to me, it was Tom Thibodeau. And I looked over there at the Lakers and Kobe was still on the floor. And so I actually said to him, "When Phil takes *that* guy out, I will take my guys out." Thibs said, "You're safe." And I said, "Not with that guy on the floor."

I was dead serious. I had obviously lost my mind, because it was a 42-point lead or something, we were in pretty good shape. But Kobe put that fear in you, man. He could run off threes and go on a run. Obviously, I was not good at math, so I was worried about him. Then, finally, Phil took him out so I could sub. It was good.

I'm very happy that Kobe (retired). He's inflicted pain on me personally, and so I'm looking forward to it. Everybody else is lying. They're saying, like, they want Kobe to keep playing and that's not true. The guy, he's inflicted pain on all of us. But on a serious note, it will be different not having him. My son Spencer was one, I think, when Kobe came into the league, and he is still playing. It's remarkable how long he's played, how well he's played, and that part you'll miss seeing. But I won't actually miss him playing, because I was always on the other side. I was always the opponent with him. No, I'm tired of seeing him play. He's played too well. I have great respect for him, but he inflicted a lot of pain on the rest of us.

Jo Jo White
Hall of Fame guard

Résumé: White had been a star at Kansas and arrived in Boston as the ninth pick in the draft in 1969. He earned an All-Star spot in his second NBA season, averaging 21.3 points per game for the Celtics, and would go on to earn seven All-Star berths in his career. White averaged 17.3 points, 4.9 assists, and 4.0 rebounds in his 12 NBA seasons, and helped Boston to championships in 1974 *and 1976, winning the Finals MVP in 1976 with averages of 21.7 points and 5.8 assists. He was inducted into the Basketball Hall of Fame in 2015.*

Kobe connection: *The Celtics-Lakers rivalry was largely dormant during White's career with the Celtics, but he was still part of the Boston family when the rivalry re-emerged in 2008, after the Celtics acquired Kevin Garnett and Ray Allen and put them with Paul Pierce. White, who called himself a "big, big fan of everything Kobe Bryant has done and meant for the league," was in attendance for the clinching Game 6 at TD Garden, and as the Celtics were being feted for their blowout defeat of the Lakers, it was a player in purple and gold who captured White's attention.*

HERE'S WHAT I remember, and I remember it very well when you mention the name Kobe Bryant. Game 6 of the Finals when the Celtics won, when they beat the Lakers that last time (in 2008), and, oh, it was quite an atmosphere at the new building there (TD Garden). It was loud, they were yelling, "Beat L.A.," and I mean, of course, the score was pretty lopsided. The Celtics won. They beat the Lakers by something like 30 or 40 points (the final margin was 39). And I remember watching that game there in my seat, and I was watching the last few moments as the clock went down and I saw Kobe Bryant. And I could see the look on his face and I thought, "Well, now, that is going to be trouble, maybe for us next year, or for somebody." I tapped the person sitting next to me, and it might have been (John) Havlicek, but I don't know for sure, and I just pointed to Kobe Bryant and the look on his face.

He is a proud man, and just a wonderful basketball player, and you know that he works so, so hard, all of the time. But he is proud, and I remember watching him walk off while all of the celebrating is going on. He was obviously in a lot of pain. I had not lost in the Finals, and the way the playoffs are now, there is a lot more of the extra, the hoopla that goes with it. I have lost playoff series that I thought we should have won. We thought we should have won in 1975, but we lost to Washington. I know how that hurts, and I would imagine it is even greater for the Finals, and especially now, with all the attention on it. You have to see the replay for two or three months after you lose, I don't know how these guys deal with that.

But I can remember saying that the look on (Bryant's) face, I knew it was that his pride was wounded. I had seen enough from him to that point to know he was not going to let that go. I think that happens with great players who can't accept losing. They forget the times they won and they remember the times they lost, and they push themselves every time they think of that loss. Of course, what happened next? The Lakers came back the next year and they won. Then they got the Celtics again in 2010, and they won again. I think he was always looking to make up for that loss. I never asked him that, but I am sure of it. You could see it in his face with that big loss that he was not going to forget anytime soon. I don't believe he did.

Tony Allen
Guard/forward

Regular Season	Games	Wins	Losses	Win %	Field Goal %	PPG	Points (High)	RPG	APG	SPG
Bryant	24	12	12	0.50	0.42	25.5	43 (3/20/06)	5.3	4.4	1.1
Allen	24	12	12	0.50	0.487	9	27 (3/22/16)	3	1.8	1.4

Playoffs	Games	Wins	Losses	Win %	Field Goal %	PPG	Points (High)	RPG	APG	SPG
Bryant	10	5	5	0.50	0.387	26.4	38 (6/13/10)	7	4.2	2.5
Allen	10	5	5	0.50	0.40	3	7 (6/8/10)	0.8	0.5	0.8

Résumé: *Allen has managed to turn in a very respectable NBA career as a defense-first player, playing 727 games over 12 years and spending much of his time in Memphis—six seasons—as a starter despite a career average of just 8.9 points per game. But he has been a five-time member of the NBA's all-defense team and is widely acknowledged as one of the best perimeter defenders in the NBA. Allen suffered a difficult torn ACL injury in his left knee in 2007, and that, in part, helped push his turn toward becoming an elite defender.*

Kobe connection: *Allen made his name most prominently for himself in the two Finals he competed in, for the Celtics in 2008 and 2010, in which he was primarily charged with guarding Bryant. In Kobe's final season, while he was accustomed to receiving gifts from opposing teams in each arena he visited, he made sure to give a gift himself—a pair of his shoes, autographed, to Tony Allen. The inscription on the shoes read, "To Tony, the best defender I ever faced!" Allen sent out a message to Bryant on Twitter, with a photo of the shoes, reading, "Salute," with the hashtag, "Respect."*

A COUPLE THINGS HAPPENED that put me in that position, defensive stopper. I hurt my knee in 2007, that was one thing, and I think I had to learn to be smarter— not to try to do everything with just being athletic, but try to be thinking out there, thinking about defense. When I came into the league, too, with the Celtics, Paul Pierce was the captain, and especially after I got hurt he tried to get me back. I had to guard him in practice every day, like, right from the beginning of my career. That was 2004, so that was a long time to be guarding him in practice, and he is not easy to deal with. I stuck him for six years. That's not easy. He does a lot of stopping and starting, and you have to be careful or you will foul him. That helped me learn to not get fouls. And then it is just preparation, just making sure you have everything right, what a guy's tendencies are going to be, and how he wants to attack and what to do to stop it. I always say, it is always right there in the film. You just have to pay attention to it.

You have to be competitive. I am not going out to score 30 points a game. I have to be a glue guy. I have to help us win with our defense. I try to guard Kobe like I guard anybody: be physical but don't foul him, stay on your feet, be competitive. I remember a game when I was a rookie. I played against him. I was starting, I had to stick with Kobe. He fouled me out in (eight) minutes. Six fouls, that fast. That was a hard moment for me, and really, I never let that moment go. I learned a lot from that. He is always going to try to get you at a disadvantage, and you just have to be strong and not let him do that. Compete with him. I had to guard him twice in the NBA Finals, and of course he was going to get his shots off, and he was going to score. But I pride myself on making it harder for him.

You know, he always said good things about me, but I always tried to just put it right out of my mind, because if you listen to that, then you're going to lose that competitive edge, and I am not about to do that. You know, Kobe being nice to you, he is just trying to make you soft. It is great to get a compliment from him, he is such a big challenge to guard. He is our era's Michael Jordan, I don't think there is any doubt about that.

James Posey

Forward

Regular Season	Games	Wins	Losses	Win %	Field Goal %	PPG	Points (High)	RPG	APG	SPG
Bryant	33	20	13	0.606	0.451	28.3	52 (2/18/03)	5.9	5.5	1.3
Posey	33	13	20	0.394	0.445	9.4	23 (1/22/02)	4.9	1.5	0.8

Playoffs	Games	Wins	Losses	Win %	Field Goal %	PPG	Points (High)	RPG	APG	SPG
Bryant	6	2	4	0.33	0.405	25.7	36 (6/10/08)	4.7	5	2.7
Posey	6	4	2	0.66	0.50	8.7	18 (6/12/08)	3.8	0.5	1.3

Résumé: *For 12 NBA seasons, Posey was a credible scorer who also happened to be a good defensive player. He averaged 8.6 points for his career and was a decent three-point shooter (34.9 percent from the arc) who peaked when he averaged 13.4 points for the 2003-'04 Grizzlies, helping that team to the franchise's first-ever playoff appearance. Two years later, Posey joined the Heat and was able to chip in as a very good perimeter shooter who could also be a defensive stopper on the perimeter. He carried that role to Boston in 2007, joining the Celtics' Big Three of Paul Pierce, Kevin Garnett, and Ray Allen and, as he had done in Miami, helping the Celtics to a title with three-point shooting and his ability to lock up foes defensively on the perimeter.*

Kobe connection: *To win those NBA Finals in 2008, Posey had to help the Celtics past the Lakers, and that meant he would have to contribute on the defensive end against Bryant, while also knocking down the occasional three-pointer. He did a very good job with both, as Kobe struggled for stretches of the series. In Boston's stunning comeback win in Los Angeles in Game 4 of that series, Posey helped hold Bryant to 17 points on 6-for-19 shooting, while Posey's clutch three-pointers (he was 4-for-8) led to 18 points and helped move the Celtics to the brink of the championship. In all, Bryant had plenty of success against Posey's teams, winning 20 of 33 matchups as Kobe averaged 28.3 points, but the job Posey did in those Finals will always be his strongest connection with Bryant.*

EVERY PLAYER WANTS to be in the Finals, of course. It is the highest level, and it is where you really get to show what you can do. You can prove yourself; it is where all eyes are on you. In Boston, we had star players there—Paul Pierce, Kevin Garnett, Ray Allen—we had great leaders there with those guys. They put their pride aside for that team, and so the rest of us sort of followed what they were doing. But the role players, we wanted to fill our roles and do our part. Me, Eddie House, guys like that. And we always had the feeling that all of us were important, that it was a true team thing, and when we went up against the Lakers we knew it was not going to be one guy who would beat them. We knew it would be Kobe Bryant who would try to do most of the damage for them, but we knew it was going to have to be all of us who helped to contain him if we were going to win a championship. It was all about winning that championship, and I tried to remind the guys of that all along. I told them when we won the East, when we beat the Pistons, that was nice, but we were now playing for a championship. We were going to have to beat the Lakers to make it all worthwhile.

I think people forget, they were the big favorites in that series. Kobe was MVP that year. I think most people and fans and media, they thought the Lakers were going to win. I think a lot of that had to do with Kobe, heading into the series I don't think a lot of people were picking us. But we were able to give him some different looks, and I think that is the important thing, you can't let him get into a rhythm. He does so much, especially when he gets on a roll. He can shoot threes, he can attack the basket, he can do all of that. So we kept giving him different looks, and you try to keep the pressure on him on the other end, too, so that you can tire him out.

You just try to control him by making him work. That was a challenge I always wanted to accept. It was not like there was trash talk or anything. It was all business, and I approached trying to guard him that way. You know, we were not the ones who got the limelight, but that was always fine with me. It was all about winning, and at the end of the day it was about winning the championship. I think in that situation you have to hit the floor as much as possible, you have to dive for the loose balls, because that's going to be the difference when you are at that stage. I had won in Miami two years before, I wanted to win in Boston, and coaching in Cleveland I want to be on that stage as much as possible.

Game 4 is the one most people remember, because we were down by so many points (24 at most) on the road, but we came back to win. That was special to me, and even though we had to make that comeback I think it was the job we did on Kobe (who was 6-for-19 from the field) that made the difference. We did not want to give him any easy shots, understanding that he is still going to make some. I think we were able to do that.

Eric Musselman

Coach

Résumé: Musselman's father, Bill, was an innovative and creative coach at the pro and collegiate levels, and Eric Musselman followed him into the coaching profession. Musselman has coached at every level of basketball, from the old Continental Basketball Association and the U.S. Basketball League to a stint in the D-League, to assistant coaching jobs with such legendary coaches as Chuck Daly, Hubie Brown, and Mike Fratello, to head NBA coaching jobs with the Kings (2006-'07) and Warriors (2002-'04), to his most recent job coaching the University of Nevada. Musselman had a record of 270-122 in the CBA, a .688 winning percentage that ranks second only to George Karl. He collected a career NBA record of 108-138 in his three seasons as a head coach.

Kobe connection: *Musselman coached against Bryant 12 times in his NBA career, and in Musselman's last NBA go-round with the Kings, Kobe managed 31.3 points and 9.5 assists in four games and won three out of the four meetings. But one of Musselman's most telling connections with Bryant occurred while he was coaching the Los Angeles D-Fenders, which operated out of the Lakers' practice facility in El Segundo. There, a late-night encounter with Kobe told Musselman much about how Bryant maintains his dominance.*

THE THING ABOUT him was, when you are on the sideline coaching against someone like that, he was just no nonsense, no emotion; he was just always focused every second of every game. He could be 2-for-20 from the field, but you knew at the end of the game he was still going to be the guy who got the ball, and he was going to try to rip your throat out.

We saw him when he was young, in those first two years, before he really was getting a lot of playing time, and you could tell he was a really good player with a lot of talent. But I just remember that third year, that was when you realized that he was going to be one of the all-time greats. We saw him in what was probably his best game up to that point, when he was just unstoppable and I think had a career high against us (38 points against Orlando). You started to get the sense that this guy was more than just good.

His work ethic is unmatched. I think that became obvious over the course of his career, and not just how hard he worked, but he seemed to be able to find whatever the flaw was in his game and correct it. So he worked hard, but he worked smart, too. His basketball IQ is really something that gets underrated, because he was able to beat you with his brains as much as with his talent and athleticism. I think whatever the things he can't do, like shoot three-pointers, that was not his strong suit, I still think he could kick ass in any generation, in any era. In our day, there is such a focus on the three-point line, guys hitting corner threes, finding the highest percentage spots, I think if he had come up in that environment, he would have been a 40 percent three-point shooter. But that was not as important when he was coming up in the league. All of his drives to the bucket, his midrange game, his transition scoring, all of that stuff he has in the bank because that was what he needed to know. If he were 25 now, he would be spending a lot more time developing that three-point shot. And he'd be great at it.

When I was coaching against him, we used to have game plans specifically designed for him. There were only a handful of guys who you felt like you needed to do that for: make a plan based only on them. It was like the Jordan Rules, but only we would call it the Kobe Rules. So with Kobe we had an approach where we would start one quarter and force everything to his left, no matter where he caught the ball. The defender was supposed to get up on his right side, on his right hip, so we knew he was going left. The next quarter, we would change it and force him to the right, just trying to throw him off guard. In the third quarter, a lot of times it was double-teaming, sending a body over to him, coming off of a non-scorer. In the fourth quarter, we would try to switch up each one of those approaches during the quarter, just play him one way, then switch it at each timeout. We tried to find a way to give him different looks but keep all of our guys on the same page, because you could not just tell one guy to force him to the left or right. You needed all five guys to be aware of where he is and where he is going.

We had all these schemes that we would try to use against him, just to give him different looks and keep him from getting too comfortable. You couldn't just play him like anyone else. He would kick your ass. He's one of the few guys who you spend your prep on a player instead of a system or a team. Your game planning was Kobe, Kobe, Kobe. He was so dominant, we knew he was going to take a high volume of shots and probably score 30, 40 points, so for us we knew we just had to take those shots and make them difficult, give them a higher degree of difficulty. We felt like if we played him the same way the whole game, he would absolutely annihilate us because he is so smart. That was the biggest thing, his basketball IQ. He was going to figure out whatever you were doing.

We had a game in Sacramento, I remember, in 2007, and Kobe had 42 points. He almost had a triple-double (ten rebounds and nine assists), and he went to the free-throw line a lot of times (20 altogether). It was at our place and it went to overtime, Mike Bibby had 38. There wasn't much defense in that game, I can tell you that. It was, he scored, Mike scored, then they came back down and four other guys watched. We had a big comeback in that game; we were down big in the fourth quarter (12 points), but we tied it up and actually took a lead late, but they managed to get it to overtime. It was entertaining for fans, I am sure, but as a coach you don't want entertaining.

The thing about Kobe I will most remember, though, came later. When I was coaching in the D-League, for the Lakers' team, we would play at the Lakers' practice facility, and there was one night that we played and I stayed late. I was in the locker room after the game. I went upstairs to the office for a little bit and did some work. Then I am getting ready to leave, I went out to the parking lot and there was nobody out there, everybody had left. All of a sudden, a car rolls up, the window slides down, and there is Kobe. He scared the crap out of me, really, a car pulls up out of the blue in a parking lot. But it was Kobe and he said, "Hey, is everyone out of there?" I asked what he meant. He said he wanted to make sure it was empty, because he wanted to go in and shoot without anyone else around. It was like 11:20 or 11:30 at night, and he must have been keeping an eye on it because he did not pull up until I came out, and I had the last car there. He did not want anyone in that gym. He did not want anyone to see him going in, he did not want any distractions. It was just him and the security guard.

You hear stories like that about a guy like Kobe wanting to shoot in some gym, or put in extra work somewhere on the road, and sometimes you wonder how true they are. But I was there, it was true. With him, believe it.

Alvin Gentry
Coach

Résumé: Gentry first broke into the NBA coaching ranks in 1988, when he became an assistant with the Spurs at age 34. He would go on to five head-coaching stints, first as an interim coach in Miami, then replacing head coach Doug Collins in Detroit for three seasons in the late 1990s. He coached the woebegone Clippers for three seasons and later took over for coach Terry Porter in Phoenix, where he coached the Suns in the run-and-gun style of one of his predecessors, Mike D'Antoni. Gentry returned to the head-coaching ranks in 2015 with the New Orleans Pelicans. He's been in charge of some rebuilding projects, which weighs down his 365-422 career record, but he has been an NBA coach in some capacity for 27 seasons.

Kobe connection: Gentry had a rather well-known exchange with Bryant in the postseason in 2010, when Kobe made a deep two-point jump shot over Grant Hill with 34 seconds to play in Phoenix, giving the Lakers a seven-point lead and effectively ending the series. Gentry tossed his hands in the air, and Bryant, standing next to Gentry after the shot went in, reached out and patted Gentry on his backside. When Bryant visited New Orleans for the final time in April 2016, Gentry was asked whether he'd be giving Kobe a gift. Gentry said, "I would like him to take that slap back that he put on my butt in 2010, when he made just a killing jump shot in that series in the Western Conference finals." But Gentry has long known of Bryant's capabilities—he was coaching the Pistons in Kobe's 1996 Summer League debut and raved after the game about Bryant's 27-point performance in that game.

I DO REMEMBER WATCHING him in his first game in Summer League; we played against them and he was just amazing. I think no one really knew what to expect, but he was just completely confident and fundamentally sound. It was in Long Beach; it was crowded, everyone was excited. Everybody knew that he was coming in, and he wanted to be the next Michael Jordan, and you could see it in the way he carried himself. He wanted to be that way. He came along at just the right time, because he came along when Michael was going to be hanging them up soon, so by the time he got bigger and more experienced, you knew he was going to be ready. But when I first saw him, I was surprised he was that good, I remember saying, you know, for a guy his age, I never saw anyone better.

He was a teenager, but it was clear he belonged in the NBA. You could see it right away, everybody who happened to be in that building could see it. I don't care how young he was.

But what I always loved about him is that he always found a way. He loved the game so much that he would always find a way to make himself better and give his team a better chance to win. You never want to see players shortchange their talent, and I think Kobe is the rare guy because he has so much talent, but he still always went above and beyond to maximize his talent.

You know, it is a long way from Summer League to where he wound up, third on the NBA scoring list, and behind two pretty good guys, Kareem Abdul-Jabbar and Karl Malone. And I saw enough of him, a lot of it up close and at my expense, in terms of how he can close out a game and deliver a win. I don't think anyone is on his level as far as being a closer; I think he is the best in the game at that. Like I said, I saw that myself an awful lot.

I really appreciate who he is. The way he approaches things. We spent time in Newport Beach, and you would see him working out in the summer, in July when everybody else is probably vacationing. But that's what drives him; that is who he is. He truly wanted to be the greatest player ever to put on a uniform, and to me he did everything he possibly could to get there. I think it will change the league a lot. When you have an appreciation for a guy with his skill level, and what he can do and the way he competes, as coaches you miss that, and as players you miss that, because it's a pretty good yardstick to measure yourself by, on where you are. Not just from a talent standpoint, but from a competitive standpoint. He will be missed. Just some of the things he has done, the highlights.

For a perimeter player to be able to go out and get 81 points in an NBA game, that's pretty unbelievable, it really is. To do it with ease, too, it wasn't something that he was forcing shots. It was pretty good rhythm.

I think anyone you would coach, you would want them to have the competitive spirit Kobe has. I think that would be true of any coach in the league, if you ask, they would say, if you could find a way to bottle the competitiveness that he had when he walked out on the court. I think the great thing for me, as a coach, I liked the fact that he was having fun in the retirement tour. I agree with (Byron) Scott on one thing, and that is, it's tough to see him go out in a situation where he is not winning. It would be great if he could do it like (Broncos Super Bowl champion quarterback) Peyton Manning. Because I think he is deserving of something like that. He is deserving of going out as a winner, if he could go out as a potential champion.

Dwyane Wade

Guard

Regular Season	Games	Wins	Losses	Win %	Field Goal %	PPG	Points (High)	RPG	APG	SPG
Bryant	20	9	11	0.45	0.436	26.1	42 (12/25/04)	4.1	4.7	1.2
Wade	20	11	9	0.55	0.455	24.3	40 (12/25/06)	4.6	6.5	1.9

Résumé: In 13 seasons with the Heat, Wade averaged 23.7 points, led the league in scoring once (in 2008-'09, when he averaged 30.2 points), and made 12 All-Star teams. He also won three NBA championships and was the Finals MVP in 2006 when the Heat upset the Mavericks by winning four straight after falling behind in the series, 0-2. Wade averaged 34.7 points in those Finals, with 7.8 rebounds and 3.8 assists, and would go on to win championships for the Heat in 2012 and 2013 before signing on to leave the Heat and join his hometown Bulls in the summer of 2016. Wade was also a member of USA Basketball's Olympics team in 2008 and led the U.S. to a gold medal with a team-high 16.0 points per game.

Kobe connection: Over the course of their careers, Bryant and Wade met 20 times, with the results just about even—Wade won 11 games to Bryant's nine. Both players obviously got ramped up playing against each other, as Kobe averaged 26.1 points and Wade averaged 24.3 in their head-to-head matchups. Early in Wade's career, the one thing he and Kobe had that most closely connected them was their relationship with big man Shaquille O'Neal, who was traded from the Lakers in 2004 after his relationship with Bryant disintegrated beyond repair. It was in their first post-trade meeting that Kobe had his best individual game against Wade, a 42-point outpouring on Christmas Day, a game won by the Heat in overtime. Two Christmases later, in 2006, Wade returned the favor, scoring 40 points of his own against the Lakers, and adding 11 assists in a big win. Despite their professional familiarity, Wade and Bryant did not become friends until they played together in the Beijing Olympics.

I FEEL THAT KOBE is the best player of our era. I have been saying, there won't be another Kobe. I really believe that.

Everybody has their moment, wants to have their moment going against a guy like him, one of the greats of the game. I have guarded Kobe so many times; we went against each other a lot on All-Star weekend. I think some of those All-Star MVP trophies he has should be at my house, because he scored a lot of those points on me. He is just a competitor and he always has been. I think everybody in the league at one point or another has idolized Kobe, no matter how good you are. A lot of us have been fans of Michael Jordan since we were growing up, but we did not get to see Michael up close the way we see Kobe now. That is a big difference.

It's cool to have a relationship with him, to learn things from him as a mentor. Having a relationship with one of my heroes, one of my role models as a basketball player, it has always meant a lot to me. To be able to pick up the phone with a guy like that, reach out to him, means a lot. It means more than the words that even he can say.

We always had a lot of respect for each other; that comes from competing against each other. Only good thing for me was, we only had to compete against each other twice a year. But we were playing together on the Olympic team (in 2008), that changed everything, 100 percent. When you see a guy daily, you get to see his work ethic, you get to see him nonstop, you get to be around him, you get to hear his knowledge of the game. You get to play with a guy, you are in the trenches with a guy. At that time, with the Redeem Team, it was important for us to get back on the right track for the USA team. That was a special team that we had, so the relationships that came out of there, myself and Kobe, you see it now with the relationship that we have. It's just a total amount of respect.

For me it was like he was the bar and you measured yourself by that bar. I remember the first time we played the Lakers, it was a blowout and they had their team at that time, the team with Gary Payton and Karl Malone. The whole game, if he was guarding me, he was backing off me, like giving me ten feet, daring me to shoot it. Like you would do with a rookie. And I did not do much to make him pay for it, I think I scored maybe ten points and did not play well at all (ten points, four-for-ten shooting, five turnovers). I think it was the next year, when we played them, he started getting a little more physical with me. He was hitting me, I was trying to hit him back. Compared to my rookie year, I was thinking, well at least he knows I am here. He is hitting me, so he knows I am here.

It kind of took off from there. He respects competitiveness. I wanted to be competitive at his level. He's a competitor. I'm competitive. We will always have that in common.

Tim Grover

Trainer

Résumé: Grover first gained fame as the trainer who helped Michael Jordan in the early 1990s, when Jordan was struggling to handle the physical play of the hard-fouling Detroit Pistons. Determined to bulk up, Jordan began seeing Grover daily, and the work he put in paid off. Jordan was able to get past the Pistons and eventually won six NBA championships, working with Grover throughout that time. Grover has since worked with several NBA stars, including Dwyane Wade and, of course, Kobe Bryant.

Kobe connection: Bryant was referred to Grover by Jordan following the Lakers' loss to the Celtics in the 2008 Finals, which saw Kobe struggle at the close of the series. In the final three games, Bryant averaged 21.3 points but shot just 33.9 percent from the field, and also averaged 4.0 turnovers. After making some adjustments in his physical regimen, Bryant returned to the top of the hill the following year, beating Orlando for the 2009 championship, then exacted some revenge on the Celtics by beating Boston in 2010.

WHEN THE LAKERS lost in the Finals in 2008, I think Kobe was really frustrated. His knees were hurting, he wanted to find a way to keep himself at his top physical shape all the way through the Finals, and he felt like he was losing the ability to do that. So Michael Jordan—I had worked with Michael in the '90s—suggested that he call me, and that was the start of me working with Kobe. The first thing we had to do was go back and look at the 2008 playoffs and see what was wrong. It was obvious: he got tired, he peaked too early, then when the Finals came, he was worn down. And he told me what he was doing, how he was working out during the playoffs because he thought it would keep his energy up. But it was the opposite. He was doing too much, and I told him he needed to work out less during the playoffs, but just make the workouts he did more intense. He had to take it easy on his body; he was trying to do too much. It is not often you have to tell a guy, hey, you're going too hard, take it easy.

But that is how Kobe was. So all through the next season we worked with him, I met with him through the year and sort of monitored what was going on with him, and we came up with a plan. It was the whole year. I think people started seeing me around him in the playoffs, because that was where it was most important. That was where we wanted to see where he was at every single day, so I think it was put out as if I had just started working with him in the playoffs. But it was that whole year. He had a great year, he took some pressure off himself, but he worked hard and made sure he was ready for the playoffs. Then he sort of unleashed in the playoffs, and his performance went up rather than down. And they won another championship. I think he is still bothered by the 2008 Finals loss, but the '09 Finals at least made up for it a little. Then he won again in 2010.

What makes him unique among the guys I have trained, and what makes him different from Michael, is that Kobe always wants to know what is going on as we are doing things. You know, I will have him increase his reps in something or decrease or change his body movement, and he will say, "OK, but why?" He wants to understand. Some people are like that, they perform better if they understand why they're doing the things they're doing. Kobe is that way, he is very cerebral. We ask our players to buy into something when they train with us, but Kobe approaches it like, he will buy in when he understands the reasoning behind it. Then he will give max effort. But before that, it will be, "Why am I eating this now? Why are we doing this or that?"

Michael would give max effort, but he would just sort of come in and say, "This is what I want." You could tell him how he could do it, and that was fine with him, he would do the work but he just wanted results; he did not need the reasons. But their work ethic was similar, they were always willing to push it as hard as they could. One thing they had in common was, when I first started working with Michael, he was at the top of his game individually, but he wanted to find a way to deal with the Pistons and how physical they were. He wanted to break through and help his team beat those guys. He could have easily been satisfied with scoring 32, 33 points a night and going to the Hall of Fame. But he wanted to win. Kobe was the same way. There was nothing wrong with going to the Finals and losing, the Celtics were a great team. But that thinking never crossed his mind. It put some pressure on me, because he hired us to get him to a championship, and I knew anything less would mean we failed.

But Kobe, one of the great things about him is that he keeps the mental side of things at the same level as the physical; he just naturally understands the connection there. He approaches all his opponents the same way. He does not want to give you any edge; he does not want to let you know you might have gotten the best of him.

The story that I have in my book, *Relentless*, from the All-Star game in 2012 in Orlando, that was the All-Star game where Kobe had his nose broken by Dwyane Wade. They were friends already. I think people made something out of nothing with that, but they were close friends going back to the Olympics in 2008. After that All-Star game, Kobe went up to Wade and talked to him, but he wanted to do it before he got any treatment. He was not going to go up to Wade with a bandage on. And it was just because, that way, Wade sees him but Bryant is still in control, like, "Yeah, this happened, but it did not hurt me, I still got this. You hit me, but I'm still here." He had a concussion and a broken nose, but he was still thinking like a competitor. That's just his personality.

Draymond Green

Forward

Regular Season	Games	Wins	Losses	Win %	Field Goal %	PPG	Points (High)	RPG	APG	SPG
Bryant	8	3	5	0.375	0.382	24.1	44 (11/16/14)	6.5	3.4	1.1
Green	8	5	3	0.625	0.419	6.9	18 (11/24/15)	5.5	2.6	1

FACING KOBE BRYANT

Résumé: It was former Laker—and fellow Michigan State Spartan—Magic Johnson who predicted stardom for Draymond Green coming out of college, but Green fell to the second round of the draft. There, the Warriors picked him up, and within two years he was playing a starting role in Golden State's championship run. In his fourth NBA season, Green earned an All-Star spot and finished the year with averages of 14.0 points, 9.5 rebounds, and 7.4 assists, and was twice the runner-up for the league's Defensive Player of the Year award.

Kobe connection: The Lakers and Warriors played eight times with both Green and Bryant on the floor, and Green won five of the matchups. Green has never played particularly well against Bryant's Lakers, averaging 6.9 points when Kobe plays and only twice cracking double-digits in scoring. He did, however, see Bryant unload for 44 points on the Warriors in November 2014, though Golden State won that game.

THINK THE THING I remember most was in my rookie year, when I first got to the league, I was finishing my pregame workout and he came out of the locker room and walked past our bench to their end. I sat on the end of our bench watching him walk. Next thing I know, I'm watching his entire workout. Before I knew it, I was supposed to be in the back doing some correctional, functional stuff. I had sat there and watched him work out for 20 minutes—his whole workout.

Just starstruck, just sitting there. I was like, "Man, that's Kobe. I've been watching him play all while I was growing up, my whole life, and I'm about to play against him." Kobe is one of those special guys, and the game may never see another player like him. Just to be around him in these last few years, it is amazing, it is history; he is one of the greatest players of all time. He's meant so much to the game. Growing up in the era that I did, Kobe was that guy. So to play in an All-Star Game with him, I mean, that's special. I grew up a Kobe fan, so it's something that's really, really special.

He has been very supportive of me, and of a lot of guys around the league. When I was struggling in the Western Conference finals against OKC, he sent me a text basically just telling me to keep going, and he said, "If making history was easy, why bother?" That stuck with me. That kind of thing means a lot coming from someone like him, someone you watched win all those championships, and who has such a great legacy and reputation in the game.

As a player, of course, you don't like going against him because you know what he can do. I did not play against him in his prime, but I know what he could do in his prime, and even when he got older he would still have one of those nights, you know? Every now and then, he would just have one of those nights and you can understand what made him so great for so long. He had a certain amount of swagger, too, so you would be watching him and he would be just cutting up somebody, right? Just scoring in all different ways, because that is what he can do. He can score inside, he can score outside, he is going to get to the free-throw line, he has the whole arsenal. And you would see him just look at his man like, "You know I am going to kill you, right?" That was the best part of watching him, just watching the way he carried himself. I think everybody in the league can learn from that.

Charles Barkley
Hall of Fame forward

Regular Season	Games	Wins	Losses	Win %	Field Goal %	PPG	Points (High)	RPG	APG	SPG
Bryant	7	5	2	0.714	0.42	16.9	27 (12/12/97)	4.7	1.1	1.3
Barkley	7	2	5	0.286	0.51	22.3	33 (11/12/96)	13.6	3.3	0.4

Résumé: Barkley, now an analyst for TNT, played 16 NBA seasons as one of the league's most outspoken and frequently controversial figures. He logged 1,073 games in his NBA career, and averaged 22.1 points and 11.7 rebounds, making 11 All-Star teams. Barkley came into the league with the Sixers, but his relationship with the team grew sour after eight seasons, and he was shipped to Phoenix. Barkley won an MVP award with the Suns in 1992-'93 and led Phoenix to the NBA Finals, though the Suns lost to the Bulls in that series in six games. He was a member of the 1992 Olympic "Dream Team" for USA Basketball and was chosen as one of the league's 50 greatest players in 1996.

Kobe connection: Barkley was a close friend of Michael Jordan during their playing careers and has compared the two as players.

Barkley saw Bryant only seven times on the court, all within the first three years of his career, and Kobe won five of them, posting an average of 16.9 points (Barkley averaged 22.3 points and 13.6 rebounds in those games). But Barkley says Bryant was not particularly outgoing during his career, though he has urged Kobe to get into broadcasting in his retirement.

ITHINK HE RETIRED at the right time; I was happy for him. He has been the ultimate competitor. It has been a privilege and an honor to watch him play. You can look back on his career, and I remember when he was young and we did not know who this kid was, how good he was going to be. You can never tell how good someone is going to be when he is 18 or 19. He struggled early on, he was not playing, he shot the air balls against Utah in the playoffs. That was the thing that, at that time, everybody saw from him. But he came back from that and he came back stronger and stronger, and you see where he wound up. It has been fun watching him develop and become the player he was. I've been blessed; I got to play against him and Jordan, who was the greatest in my opinion. Larry Bird, Magic Johnson, Dr. J, Patrick Ewing, all of those guys. Kobe is right there or even better. So, it's been an honor.

Kobe is a guy who, over the years, I don't think he wanted to let anyone get to know him; he is very private. He's a unique guy, a quiet guy, I am not sure anybody knows him very well. He is always cordial, he is a really nice guy to me, but he keeps his distance. He is one of the greatest players ever to play the game, but he had such a different approach to the game. He just wants to play basketball, he does not want all the other stuff. He is not going to go fishing with you. He wants his teammates to show and play and be ready to play; he has a one-track mind as far as that goes. I can respect that. He is a loner. I don't know why. I don't know if he did not like dealing with all the negative attention with him vs. Shaq, or him vs. Phil, or whatever it was. But he did not want to put himself out there.

It's too bad about the Lakers when he was at his peak with Shaq. I think what you learn later on in life is that you really want to play with other great people and players. If Kobe and Shaq could have put all that inside and get along, they would have been so great, they would have won more championships. They would have to rewrite the record book. In the last year, as he was playing, once he decided he was going to retire and he made the announcement of it, I think Kobe changed, I do think he became more open. I think he has a better personality. I think he is more interesting and fun than he lets on, really. But I always thought it was interesting because of the way he really did just keep himself all about basketball. All of L.A. loved him, but he was not really interested in that. He just wanted to play. And he was obviously one of the greatest players of all time.

PART 4:

LEGACY

"**H**E HAD A great career and he did a lot of things for basketball. But I don't even know if he knows all the things he did, all the people all over the world who watched him and loved him and have his jersey." –*Zaza Pachulia*

WITH A GREAT player like Bryant—not just in the NBA, but in any sport—there comes a point in his career at which the events and incidents that take place around him get funneled into the question: what will this mean to his legacy?

At several points here in the tail end of Bryant's career, that has been a concern. The Achilles tendon injury he suffered in 2013 sapped him of some of his athleticism, and he never really seemed to recover fully. The contract he signed ($48.5 million) for the final two seasons of his career hamstrung the Lakers' payroll and their ability to improve the roster during the end of his tenure. The way the Lakers finished, with two straight years of the worst records in franchise history (21 wins in 2014-'15, 17 wins the following year), were a blemish on his overall accomplishments.

At least conventional wisdom held that they would be. When Bryant announced his retirement in November 2015, though, he seemed to finally relax, to let up on the suspicious treatment of fans and media, to take it easier on his teammates in practices, to be more open and expansive in showing his personality and engaging with other players and fan bases around the league. It was a much different look for Bryant, and it suited him. It carried right through the emotional final game at the Staples Center, when he scored 60 points on 50 shots in his career finale and received an outpouring of thanks, applause, and love from the home fans he'd entertained for 20 years.

At that point, no one cared about whether his contract or the Lakers' poor record affected his legacy. By the end of the season, Bryant had adjusted the general opinion of himself. His legacy was in better shape than ever.

He will leave behind a legacy that will continue to show up in the coming years. During his farewell tour, Bryant made it a point to seek out and offer his advice and encouragement to some of the most promising young stars in the game, including Giannis Antetokounmpo of the Bucks and Karl-Anthony Towns of Minnesota. His approach to the game continues to inspire budding young players, as well as fans internationally, whom Bryant has long courted—making a special point to reach out through Olympic bids with Team USA—and who have responded in droves. By the time it was over, once Bryant wrapped up his 20-year career, he had turned former foes into fans, had created the most memorable hoops farewell in league history, and had left the game representing the kind of player the modern game seems to have abandoned: the do-it-all perimeter wing, the kind of player with roots in guys like Oscar Robertson, Dominique Wilkins, and Michael Jordan.

In fact, as Wilkins said, "The kind of player I was, we are not going to see that anymore. Kobe is the last one."

Giannis Antetokounmpo
Guard/forward

Regular Season	Games	Wins	Losses	Win %	Field Goal %	PPG	Points (High)	RPG	APG	SPG
Bryant	2	1	1	0.50	0.37	18.5	22 (12/15/15)	4	4	0.5
Antetokounmpo	2	1	1	0.50	0.643	21	27 (2/22/16)	9	7.5	1.5

Résumé: *Antetokounmpo ranks among the most exciting NBA stars in the post-Bryant era. His build and demeanor alone have gradually earned for him a spot as a singular player in the NBA, a 7-footer who can handle the ball well enough to play point guard, but who is big enough to guard power forwards. He's full of raw talent, and in his third season in the NBA averaged 16.9 points, 7.7 rebounds, and 4.3 assists at the young age of 21. Known as the Greek Freak, Antetokounmpo has been establishing himself as a future star with the Bucks.*

Kobe connection: *On February 22, 2016, Antetokounmpo had his most memorable game of the season, facing off against Bryant's Lakers and posting a triple-double, with 27 points, 12 rebounds, and ten assists, adding four blocked shots and three steals for good measure. It was especially meaningful for Antetokounmpo, who grew up in Greece and had access to a limited number of NBA games as a child, many of which featured Bryant and the Lakers, making Kobe one of his role models. Bryant was so impressed that, after the game, he sought out Antetokounmpo to offer advice on getting the most out of his talent. "He has the talent to be a great* *player," Kobe told reporters at the time. Antetokounmpo has held the advice of Bryant closely since then.*

WHEN I WAS growing up in Greece, we did not get to see that many NBA games, but I always wanted to watch as many as I could, and a lot of times Kobe Bryant would be on; it would be the Lakers. I don't think I can say I tried to play like him, because I knew how great he was and I just wanted to learn a little bit from watching him, learn whatever I could. You know, like, take some secrets from him. When you play against him, he is always trying to get the advantage, and he does not need too much advantage to be able to take the ball and go, to go to shoot it or to go to dribble to the rim. When you try to guard him you don't even think you are giving him an advantage, but he is very smart, so he finds the advantage even if it is one inch. He can get you off balance and then he is gone.

But it meant a lot to me when we played them in his last year, because he said he wanted to talk to me. It was really great because it was my first time playing against Kobe, and I really recognize what he did in the past years. For sure, I am going to miss him. I think everyone is going to miss him. It is going to be hard for him not playing for the next coming years, but it was a great experience just being able to play with him and against him. He's one of my role models, and I always watched him when I was younger. I think if you are a young basketball player

141

in Europe, pretty much anywhere in Europe, you might not know all the players, but you know Kobe; you have seen him.

For him to acknowledge me, that is a great feeling. He wanted to talk to me, he pointed to me after our game. He told me I had a chance to be great, but I had to work hard for it. He told me I had the ability and the intelligence, but that would not matter if I did not work hard. He said how my off-season is going to be, how it should be, it should be sacrifices. If Kobe Bryant tells you this, of course you are going to listen. Of course I am going to try to do what he told me to do. There are a lot of guys who play hard in this league, so he said to be great you have to be one of them, and you have to play even harder than them. I was surprised he wanted to give me this advice, but I will not forget it.

Khris Middleton
Forward/guard

Regular Season	Games	Wins	Losses	Win %	Field Goal %	PPG	Points (High)	RPG	APG	SPG
Bryant	2	1	1	0.50	0.37	18.5	22 (12/15/15)	4	4	0.5
Middleton	2	1	1	0.50	0.355	17	18 (2/22/16)	2	5	2

Résumé: Middleton was a second-round pick from Texas A&M in 2009 and had to scrap to keep his NBA career alive. He was originally chosen by the Pistons but blossomed in Milwaukee after he was included in the trade that sent Brandon Jennings from the Bucks to the Pistons. Middleton is regarded as one of the best perimeter defenders in the league. In his fourth NBA season, he averaged 18.2 points and 4.2 assists and has made himself a reliable three-point shooter, making 40.0 percent for his career.

Kobe connection: *Middleton faced Bryant twice during Kobe's final NBA season, with Kobe scoring 18.5 points and shooting 37.0 percent from the field in the two games. Middleton had his struggles in the matchup, too, averaging 17.0 points on 35.5 percent shooting, as the Bucks and Lakers split the series. Middleton says he grew up with Bryant and Michael Jordan as his favorite players, pointing out that Kobe missed more shots in his career than any other player but still persevered and kept finding ways to score.*

I AM A HUGE Kobe Bryant fan. He is one of the reasons I love to watch the game and play the game. He inspires me to be the best player I can be, and to do everything I can do to succeed on the court. I would say I started watching him during the first championship run. I was a big Michael Jordan fan, a big Tracy McGrady fan, too, so just watching those guys, I love the way they competed and the way they played the game. One of the big things I remember about watching Kobe early on was the air balls he shot in Utah in the playoffs in 1997. But each time he came back shooting. That just shows you, you can fail, but you still have got to keep shooting. You still have to have confidence in yourself, you still have to keep trying. It was the biggest stage he had ever been on and he fell, but he came back even stronger from it. He went and dedicated himself to practicing so that would not happen again.

This year was my first year playing against him, and it was a good experience. You could see how he was thinking about the game the whole time, how he was setting up his defenders and getting his teammates into the spots they were supposed to be in. He talks a lot on the court, I mean not talking trash really, but just as a leader, telling everyone where they are supposed to be. He communicates with his teammates, and I really never saw anyone approach things that way as much as he does. He is always telling them what he sees out there. I think that should be important for any player who wants to be a leader on his team. You know, I think a lot of us will miss him, because if you look up to him, it makes it easier to follow his lead when you actually get to play against him.

What makes him tough to deal with as a defender is that he has a whole set of moves he can go to that no one else can match; he has more and more moves that he can go to. Most guys have a move, then the countermove that they go to. Kobe has countermoves to his countermoves. That is tough to guard, because you can read his move and cut it off, but he is going to go right into another without missing a beat. He is not even thinking about it, he is just reacting. He has practiced this stuff so much, he has been in every situation, he is just playing the game. It's like a computer in his head that just goes through all the options and lets one lead to the next one, until he is in position for the shot he wants.

It's experience, it's what he works out with in practice, so it comes easy in games. That is tough to guard, and he can finish on you, he can shoot jumpers on you, he can score coming off screens, he can score in the post, he can score when he is being double-teamed, sometimes triple-teamed—he can score in every way you can think of. He finds a way to make a play. Without him in the league, it is really up to the rest of us to take all of those things he could do and learn them, carry them on.

Will Barton
Guard

Regular Season	Games	Wins	Losses	Win %	Field Goal %	PPG	Points (High)	RPG	APG	SPG
Bryant	7	4	3	0.571	0.504	27	47 (4/10/13)	4.4	3.4	1.4
Barton	7	3	4	0.429	0.434	12.4	25 (12/22/15)	5.1	1.7	0.6

Résumé: *Barton was buried deep on the bench for his first two-plus seasons in Portland, but when he was traded to Denver in 2015, he began to take off. He was outstanding as a sixth man with the Nuggets in 2015-'16, averaging 14.4 points and 5.8 rebounds. He ranked fifth in Most Improved Player voting that season, and fourth in Sixth Man of the Year voting.*

Kobe connection: *Barton has been on the floor against Bryant seven times and has been a witness to some of Kobe's biggest*

*late-career games, including a 40-point burst in February 2013
and a 47-point, eight-rebound, five-assist performance two months
later—a masterwork in which Bryant memorably swatted away
a fast-break dunk attempt by Barton. Two days after that game,
Kobe suffered a torn Achilles tendon against Golden State.*

I**REMEMBER FACING HIM** during my rookie year; it was
the end of the season, and I got a chance to start against the
Lakers. I was a big fan of Kobe growing up, so I thought the
chance to match up against him was going to be really special,
just because I had always watched him and I wouldn't say I
patterned my game after him or anything like that, I just liked
the way he competed and the way he always gave everything he
had. He was so competitive, and I watched him win all five of
those championships.

I was in Portland at the time I got the start against him. We
had some injuries (starter Wesley Matthews had a bad ankle),
so I had to step in and be a starter. It was big for me, just
because, I mean, it was Kobe, and I was not really playing that
much in Portland; we had too many guys in front of me. So
that was tough from the beginning, because I am a rhythm
player. I need to get into a rhythm in order to get going, and I
had not been playing much. But I felt like I was ready for it. I
mean, as much as you can be ready to go up against Kobe Bryant for an entire game.

Getting out there, Kobe was really locked in. We were playing at home and we got off to a lead, but Kobe was making everything, he was keeping them in the game in the first half. There was a play, the one everyone remembers, that play where I got a steal and I was able to get the ball and turn for a fast break; there was no one in front of me. Kobe got back and was there in the paint and I went up on one side, I was on his left side. I went up before him, so I thought I would have a dunk on the fast break. But he came over and got his left hand over and knocked it away. I never thought he would be able to block it with his left hand like that. He trash talks a little bit, and he did on that one. But you know, he was not supposed to be that athletic anymore. That play was, like, he's still got it every now and then.

He is an assassin, man. Every play, he is in attack mode. I think he had (47) points that night. That was typical Kobe. Even when there are plays that are not actually drawn for him, once he touches the ball, he is in play. He is trying to score, he is trying to make a play for someone. People don't understand, defenses in the NBA are so good. Someone who can make it look easy like Kobe does, that's incredible. He really has no weaknesses. That always stood out to me. Just how talented he is, how aggressive he is. You've really got to lock in the way he does, it is an amazing thing. It is something that all of us should try to continue. We can't all be Kobe, but we can give the effort that he gives.

Adam Silver
NBA commissioner

Résumé: Silver had long been groomed by former commissioner David Stern to be his successor in that role, having joined the NBA executive office in 1992 and worked his way up through the league ranks as the NBA's chief of staff and the head of NBA Entertainment, among other titles, before becoming Stern's deputy commissioner in 2014.

Kobe connection: Silver has overseen the waning years of Bryant in the NBA but has also worked with him to find new and innovative roles under the NBA umbrella as Bryant begins retirement. Speaking in April 2016, Silver said of Kobe, "I'm sure this is not the last chapter for him, in terms of the NBA. He's talked a lot about all kinds of things, but he said he'd be particularly interested in doing something around media." He also addressed the impact Bryant has had on the NBA as a global entity during the Toronto All-Star game.

I'D SAY, FROM a personal standpoint, I've watched his game since the day he came into this league. I don't think there is any doubt that he'll go down as one of the greatest players to ever play this game. I'd say from a global impact, in addition to being a great player, I think because he was raised for much of his childhood in Italy, because he speaks several languages, I think because he was particularly interested in learning about other cultures, I think that he's had almost—in addition to being a great player—he's punched way above his weight in terms of the impact he's had on the global expansion of the NBA.

I was in China with him for the 2008 Olympics in Beijing. That was amazing, the number of people he touched. I mean, he made a decision that he wanted to get out and about, the number of events he went to, the amount of time that he takes personally blogging with Chinese companies, directly to Chinese fans that he has a relationship with. In fact, we had a business conference, we call it our Technology Conference (at All-Star weekend) in Toronto, and Kobe spoke to the audience there, and he talked about sort of how he saw the NBA as a global property, and the fact that because of his own curiosity he had gone—the way he had gone about talking directly to his fans throughout the world.

I'd say Kobe, his emergence, came about sort of in the beginning of the days of a strong digital media presence of the NBA. That's now been complemented by the enormous social media community, and I think Kobe's been at the center of that. So he will be missed in the league. I know, though, because I spoke directly to him about this, I think after he takes a little bit of time to decompress, he's going to be looking for ways to stay directly involved in the game of basketball.

Zaza Pachulia
Center

Regular Season	Games	Wins	Losses	Win %	Field Goal %	PPG	Points (High)	RPG	APG	SPG
Bryant	18	12	6	0.66	0.449	24.7	41 (11/1/09)	4.8	4.7	1.6
Pachulia	18	6	12	0.33	0.531	8.1	18 (11/13/15)	7.1	1.3	0.7

Résumé: *Pachulia was a second-round pick by the Magic in 2003 but still managed to hang on in the NBA for 13 seasons—playing for four teams, mostly in Atlanta—and signed on for a 14th year with the Golden State Warriors. He is known more for his hard picks and physical style of play rather than for his statistics, and his scoring average of 7.1 points (with 6.0 rebounds) reflects that. Pachulia remains immensely popular in his home country of Georgia and owns a hotel and restaurants there.*

Kobe connection: *Pachulia has played against Bryant 18 times in his career—he once saw him put up 41 points against his Hawks in a November 2009 game in Los Angeles—and though he finds chasing Bryant in pick-and-rolls to be especially difficult, Pachulia has an appreciation for how Kobe has helped bring basketball to the world stage and has particular knowledge of how love for Bryant has spread throughout Europe.*

FOR ME, WHAT I always notice when I go back home to Georgia or I go and travel around Europe, as many great

European players as there are in the league, players like Dirk Nowitzki and Tony Parker, it is always the Kobe Bryant jerseys you see. People in Europe, people around the world all know Kobe and they want his jersey; they want to watch him play. You can just walk around and see it.

I think people know he grew up in Italy and he travels around a lot. He talks to people, and he is very good at spreading basketball, being an ambassador for basketball. I think in the U.S. some people love Kobe, some people hate him. But around the world, everybody loves him. Everybody loves how he plays, how his talent is, how he shows complete effort all the time, and his style of playing the game. But everybody loves that he knows about the world, too. He asked me once where I was from, and I told him Georgia. A lot of times, guys just think it is the state, the U.S. Georgia. But he knows where it is, and told me he wants to go there someday. You know, I think he would like it.

For me, he is such a tough player, because usually when I see him it is in pick-and-roll, and I have to decide what to do, I have to cover my man, but I have to stay in front of Kobe, too, and it is not easy because he will take advantage if you don't do it right. He will go right past your defense and dunk the ball if you don't cover it right. But even if you do, he is a good shooter, and he can make the shot even with defenders on him and guarding him. That is what makes him special and different; he can keep scoring even when you are guarding him like the coach says to guard him. He reads the play so well, he knows what you are going to do most of the time. Sometimes you might go back in a timeout, and the coach is yelling at your teammate because he let Kobe Bryant score. But I don't know how you can get mad because Kobe Bryant scored. He does it so much, he is so good at it. I can't see getting mad about that.

He had a great career, and he did a lot of things for basketball. But I don't even know if he knows all the things he did, all the people all over the world who watched him and loved him and have his jersey.

Jerry Colangelo
Executive and owner

Résumé: *Colangelo first became involved with the Phoenix Suns in 1968, working as the team's first general manager before eventually working his way to an ownership stake, which he sold in 2004. He was later brought in by the Sixers as an adviser to the franchise. But beginning in 2005, he became better known as the executive director of USA Basketball, taking over in the wake of the team's embarrassing performance in the 2004 Olympics, and turned the program around, beginning an era in which the U.S. lost just one game in ten years and took four straight gold medals in international tournaments.*

Kobe connection: *As an owner of Phoenix in the 1990s, Colangelo and the Suns considered drafting Bryant coming out of high school in the 1996 draft, but Kobe was gone by the time Phoenix's pick came up. The Suns would go on to feel some pangs of regret on that* *front, as Bryant cost the team a chance to play in the 2010 Finals when he sank a dagger of a jumper in Game 6, sealing the win and paving the way to the West championship. Beyond their Lakers-Suns division rivalry, Colangelo and Bryant got to know each other better over the course of two Olympics runs: in Beijing in 2008, and again in London in 2012. Getting Bryant on board with USA Basketball would prove to be one of the turning points in righting the program.*

It was really great to get Kobe involved with Team USA. I think he really was able to set an example for a lot of the younger guys. After I took charge, we wanted to start over with USA Basketball, and Kobe Bryant was a big part of that. He never had any ego or anything like that. He wanted to be just part of the team, and it was never something where he was worried about how many shots he took or how much he was playing. He trusted Coach K completely. Because he was willing to do that, because here was Kobe Bryant and he was willing to sacrifice and acquiesce and be part of the team, he set an example that everyone, from one through 12, everyone would follow.

Before the Olympics, we had to qualify in the North Americas tournament in Las Vegas (in 2007), and I remember during a game against Brazil, he was guarding Leandro (Barbosa, of Brazil), and Kobe got his hand on a ball and he hit the floor trying to get the ball back. I thought that said a lot about him and about his approach. Everyone on that team gave great effort.

He is bigger than life, and that was really true in 2008 when we went to Beijing. Even before that, when we were doing the tour before the Olympics started, he was larger than life because there would be all these people who would come out just to see him, and he had such a good demeanor and connection to them. He was very patient, but he was also very curious; he wanted to ask questions, too. I think he was curious about the culture where he was, so it was a two-way street. He was interested in them and they were interested in him. He was the Pied Piper. We went to Macau; everywhere we went in China, he was the one everyone wanted to see, people would be lined up to see him. I had seen Olympic teams before that and since then, but I never saw anything really like that. He has one reputation for how he deals with people, but when you see him up close, you realize he is a much more open person than that.

As an NBA player, he is the same way, I don't think we have seen a lot like him. In Phoenix, we had him in for a workout before that draft, and he was very impressive even at his age. We were picking in the middle of the first round, and, quite honestly, we wanted to pick him. But the Lakers had a deal worked out with Charlotte before we got the chance to draft him, and he winds up going to L.A. and our other choice was still there—Steve Nash. So I guess you could say it worked out for everyone. It was a really good draft that year. But Kobe, the talent he had and the work he put in, he was one of a kind.

He is one of the greatest players ever to play the game. Over his career, the number of shots he made when it mattered most, I think that is how people will remember him. When you get down to the end of the game, and it is the last shot, he has as good a track record as anybody. I would want him taking that shot. He is going to make it.

Karl-Anthony Towns
Center/forward

Regular Season	Games	Wins	Losses	Win %	Field Goal %	PPG	Points (High)	RPG	APG	SPG
Bryant	3	1	2	0.33	0.397	24.3	38 (2/2/16)	3.3	2.3	1.7
Towns	3	2	1	0.66	0.605	18	26 (12/9/15)	12	1.3	0

Résumé: *Towns was the No. 1 pick, by the Timberwolves, in the 2015 draft out of Kentucky and showed why during his first season, in which he won the Rookie of the Year Award unanimously after averaging 18.3 points and 10.5 rebounds playing in all 82 games. Towns is a freakish athlete; for a 7-footer he was exceptionally efficient in his first season. He shot 54.2 percent from the field and showed promise as a perimeter shooter, setting him up to be the ideal modern player for the 2010s and into the 2020s.*

Kobe connection: *Bryant and Towns first met when Towns was playing for the Dominican Republic's national team, at age 16. Towns remembers Bryant as being supportive then and has been grateful for the support and encouragement he has received from Kobe since. There is a sense of what might have been with Towns and Bryant. Had the Lakers won the top overall pick in 2015, rather than being left with No. 2, they would have taken Towns first overall. Towns did average 18.0 points and 12.0 rebounds in three* *games against the Lakers in 2015-'16, but Kobe managed a memorable night with 38 points in his final meeting against Minnesota.*

I THINK YOU CAN'T help but notice, when you are on the court with him, that it is a little different because of all that he has accomplished. His greatness, everyone knows it. The first time I went against him, I remember playing him for the Dominican National team in 2012, when they were getting ready for Team USA to go to the Olympics. I was only 16 then. I was a skinny kid, and of course I had watched him when I was growing up. But it's a lot different being on the floor with him, even when you are that young. He is a legend, of course. He has done everything. To be able to go against him and guard him, it meant a lot. And it meant a lot for my confidence because it was Kobe, it was the best players in the world. I got to talk to Kobe after that game, and he told me to just keep working hard. Keep working hard. Again, it really meant a lot coming from him.

I got to play against him a few times, and there will be a lot of players who never have that opportunity. The last time we saw him he scored 38, and really, that was vintage Kobe. He and Andrew (Wiggins) were going back and forth in that game, but I think Kobe scored like the last eight or nine points of the game. He drew some fouls and made his free throws, and they won it. But that shows you, he is someone who can close out games. It was vintage Kobe, one last time.

I have worked tremendously hard to get where I am. I pushed myself to the limit, and I have tried to do that every night. I know that is the way Kobe approached it, all the stories you hear about him and how hard he worked. It was a thrill to be able to be out there against him, and every time we saw him he would give me more advice and tell me to keep pushing. He is a good guy and a good friend of mine now, and just to see him go about things the way he did was really humbling. It is funny because I feel like I came a long way from the first time I played against him to the last time. But I think he really cares about the league and about what it is going to be like after him, and I think he wants to make sure it is in good hands, that kind of thing. I am always going to be grateful for that. He is a legend.

Isaiah Thomas

Guard

Regular Season	Games	Wins	Losses	Win %	Field Goal %	PPG	Points (High)	RPG	APG	SPG
Bryant	10	4	6	0.40	0.411	27.3	39 (11/4/14)	6.7	4.7	1.6
Thomas	10	6	4	0.60	0.554	15.8	26 (4/3/16)	1.9	4.5	0.7

Résumé: Thomas was the last player selected—60th overall—in the 2011 NBA Draft and has come a long way since. He earned his first All-Star spot playing for the Celtics in 2015-'16, averaging a career-high 22.2 points, with 6.2 assists, to lead his team to a 48-win season. Prior to Boston, Thomas played three seasons in Sacramento and part of a season in Phoenix, and carries a career average of 17.1 points per game.

Kobe connection: *Thomas is one of the young rising stars Bryant has pulled aside to offer advice and guidance. Thomas says he grew up a fan of Kobe and relates a story from his rookie year, in which he had his first not-so-successful run-in with Bryant.*

MY FIRST YEAR, when I was with the Kings, (coach) Paul Westphal had a rule in practice that no one was allowed to back me down, because I had good hands and they always turned the ball over. So our first game was against Kobe and the Lakers, and he subbed me in. He looked at me and he said, "You got Kobe. Remember, nobody can back you down." And I said, "Man, don't lie to me!" I mean, that's Kobe. He was trying to hype me too much. But that is probably the best memory I have going against Kobe, because I got on him in that game, and the first three times out he backed me down three straight possessions and scored on me. And I am just laughing, all the way down. That was my first game, that was my best memory.

But one thing he did, he came and sat down and talked, just me and him, for like 20 minutes, and it was probably the best talk I've ever had. He told me this story about how a lion seeks food, whatever he's going to kill and eat, and you know how many bugs are on the lion's eyes and the gnats that are on his body? He's so locked in on that zebra that he doesn't get distracted by anything else. He said if you get distracted by little things, then you're not as locked in as you think you are. He told me to be a lion. And that's going to stick with me the rest of my life. He even said, "If you need to know how to guard somebody, I know how to defend everyone, so just let me know."

That is really an honor. Kobe Bryant is a guy I looked up to since I was a little kid, but he was trying to just give me some advice. Of course I am going to listen, it is Kobe Bryant. He's the greatest player of my generation. He is the closest thing there is to Michael Jordan, and he is right on that level. He carries himself like Michael Jordan, he has the same demeanor, he is a Hall of Famer. He is somebody that I've looked up to all my life, and the fact I got to share a court with him before he retired, that is really an honor for me, and the fact that he was willing to give me some advice, I will never forget that.

Metta World Peace

Forward

Regular Season	Games	Wins	Losses	Win %	Field Goal %	PPG	Points (High)	RPG	APG	SPG
Bryant	20	15	5	0.75	0.481	27.6	42 (1/4/07)	5.7	6.1	2
World Peace	20	5	15	0.25	0.375	16.7	28 (3/14/06)	5	2.9	2.7

Playoffs	Games	Wins	Losses	Win %	Field Goal %	PPG	Points (High)	RPG	APG	SPG
Bryant	7	4	3	0.571	0.453	27.4	40 (5/6/09)	5	3.7	2
World Peace	7	3	4	0.429	0.381	15.6	25 (twice)	5.3	4	1.1

Résumé: World Peace, formerly known as Ron Artest, has long been one of the most controversial players in the league, earning 14 suspensions from the league office in his 16-year career, including a 72-game suspension as a result of the 2004 brawl that took place between the Pacers, Pistons, and fans at the Palace of Auburn Hills late in a game. But World Peace also was a rugged and outstanding defensive player who honed his offensive game, earned an All-Star berth in 2003-'04 (when he was also the league's Defensive Player of the Year), and averaged 20.5 points per game during his most productive year, in Sacramento, in 2007-'08.

Kobe connection: After an especially rugged and tense playoff series— elbows were thrown, and there was a face-to-face confrontation— against Bryant and the Lakers while he was with the Rockets in 2009, World Peace left Houston and joined Kobe and the Lakers the following year. That season, the Lakers beat the Celtics in a seven-game thriller of a Finals, and World Peace earned his only NBA championship ring. After a season overseas, World Peace returned in 2015-'16 to join the Lakers and was on the bench for Bryant's dramatic final NBA game, in which he scored 60 points on 50 shot attempts.

WITH EVERYTHING THAT Kobe and I went through when we were playing together, when we were playing against each other, I was just so excited to be there for his last game, to be on the bench and cheering for him. I think I cheered so much I hurt my own head. But it was such a good feeling in the place because everybody knew what was going on, and everybody just wanted to show appreciation for Kobe and what he did for all the years he played. He was the man for so long in the NBA, and he affected a lot of people, guys in the league now and kids watching and everybody. It was a really great thing to be there for the last game because everybody was feeling the same thing, a little nervous and excited and just wanting to watch him. I was going to cheer him no matter what, and I was yelling as loud as I could. We knew the game plan was going to be to let him get the ball and shoot it. Let him shoot. Let him have the opportunity; I mean, he did not have to save himself. He could be as tired as he wanted.

I did not talk to him before the game, I don't know what was in his head, I can't imagine. He had to be nervous. I was nervous. He actually did not get off to a great start, but I think everyone knew he was going to keep shooting. He missed his first few shots, and I thought it might be a long night. But then he scored a little and got it going, and it was, like, he got it up to ten points in a few minutes and I thought, "OK, he is going to get 20 tonight." Then he got to 15 or 20 and I said, "OK, he is going to get to 30." Then he kept scoring and he had 25, and I said, "Oh, he is going to get 40 tonight." And that is how it was, for everybody, because he just kept getting better and better, and

I thought I would just stop counting, because every time I set an expectation of this many points or that many points he went above the expectation. He surpassed everyone's expectation, and that's why by the end everybody was going crazy. I never heard it that loud in there. Everybody in L.A. was just showing him a lot of love for all the years he was there. I was in awe.

He probably got tired in that third and fourth quarter. He took 50 shots and no one does that. But he did not give up. He wanted to go out on top. Utah was trying to defend him, but you could tell they did not really know what to do because he was taking it on his own. He was attacking. That's what you do; when you see a weakness, you continue to go and push and push. That is something that Kobe has always done. I have seen Kobe do unbelievable things, but that is because a lot of people don't know that he is sometimes in the gym at like four in the morning. Everybody else is sleeping; everybody he goes against in the NBA, they are in their bed, but he is in the gym working hard. He just does that, it is where he wants to be.

Playing with Kobe teaches you how to dig deeper, and that goes for all the players on the team, even the guys at the end of the bench and the rookies. He will yell at guys in practice if he thinks they are not giving 100 percent. A lot of people don't want to do that, they are afraid to dig deep and sacrifice; but when you play with Kobe, you see him doing that all the time, so you are going to have to do that, too; he is going to push that out of you. Kobe has done that, and you can see it with the championships he has won.

Everybody can say they are champions because they took what they could from Kobe Bryant. I got my ring because of Kobe. I owe him that. It is hard for some teammates because he could be hard on them, but he always wanted what was best for them and what was best for the team. Sometimes he needed to be not as hard on his teammates because he could not understand that not everyone works that hard. Not everyone is like him. But he was the reason I worked so hard when I got to the Lakers. I got that from him. He could still get his teammates to push themselves harder and harder. I think people who say he is selfish don't understand; he just wants what is best for the team.

We had some confrontation, but we did not ever talk about it. The only time it comes up is when someone else asks about it. Because we know what happens in a game like that, it does not matter after. It should not matter. I don't keep worrying about what happened in this game or that game, and Kobe does not, either. Me and Kobe are competitors. When we competed against each other, we went toe-to-toe and we were not there to be friends; we both knew that. It's competition, that is how it is supposed to be. We are not made like that, we don't apologize. We just play hard and that's it. Kobe does not care who it is against. You can feel the fire when you're in the room with him. It does not matter who he is playing, or whether it is in a game or at the end of practice playing one-on-one when you are on his team. He don't care. He wants to win. But when it is over, he is not going to keep worrying about if you hit him or he hit you.

So I knew, last game, he was going to be ready for that game. He lived up to it. I said it was the greatest night in NBA history, and I still think it is.

Dominique Wilkins
Hall of Fame forward

Regular Season	Games	Wins	Losses	Win %	Field Goal %	PPG	Points (High)	RPG	APG	SPG
Bryant	3	1	2	0.33	0.6	13.3	19 (1/29/97)	1.3	1	1
Wilkins	3	2	1	0.66	0.509	28	28 (three times)	10	2.3	1

Résumé: *Wilkins was one of the best dunkers in the NBA, known as the Human Highlight Film over the course of his 15-year career. He earned nine All-Star spots, led the league in scoring in 1985-'86 (with 30.3 points), and won two of his famed appearances in the NBA's Slam Dunk Contest, in 1985 and 1990. Following a draft-day trade from Utah in 1982, Wilkins spent most of his career with the Hawks, leading the team to the playoffs eight times. He closed his career bouncing around with the Clippers, Celtics, Spurs, and Magic, as well as two stints starring in Europe. He is 13th on the NBA's all-time scoring list with 26,668 points and was inducted into the Basketball Hall of Fame in 2006.*

Kobe connection: *Wilkins faced Bryant three times at the tail end of his career, scoring 28 points in all three meetings, when Kobe was a rookie and Wilkins was with San Antonio. But Wilkins and Bryant would become longtime friends after Wilkins's retirement, as Kobe sought out help for coping with the vagaries of the league and, also, for his winning entry in the Slam Dunk Contest. Wilkins and Bryant would later be brought together by* *a different bond: in April 2013, Bryant tore his Achilles tendon, an injury Wilkins, too, had suffered in 1992. Wilkins had been 32 at the time and made a successful comeback from the injury, though Kobe was 35 when he returned from the injury and was never quite the same.*

WHEN I PLAYED against him, he was just so young. I was at the end of my career; I was in San Antonio, and this was the time when they were just starting with drafting kids out of high school. A lot of older guys, we were not going to worry about a kid who was 18 years old, you know? There was Kevin Garnett the year before, he was a big guy, though. But Kobe was a perimeter player, so of course a lot of us were skeptical, a teenager coming right into the NBA. I think he had a lot to prove right away, and he really carried himself that way. But we were skeptical, a lot of us.

Obviously, we were wrong on that. What a great career he had, and, really, it was sad to watch him wrap it up, because I think it represented something for the players of my generation who played the way I did, or Michael Jordan did or Clyde Drexler did. I like to say Kobe is the "Last of the Mohicans." That's what I called him. Because he's the last guy who is going to play like that all the time. You know, the game has changed. You look at the shooting guards, the small forwards who are in the league now, and they are guys who shoot from the three-point line and maybe play some defense. But they are not really guys who can do it all. You won't see another player like that again. In terms of competitiveness, the style of play, playing the game at a very high level. You don't see that kind of guy very often, and I think the way the game is now, you won't see it again.

He is such a fundamentally sound player. He just knows what he is going to do before he starts to do it. He is going to go through a series of moves, and he is going to get you in the position he wants you to be in before he decides to go ahead and get his shot. He will post you up, face you up. He just wants to take the high percentage shot, and if that is posting you up for taking a fadeaway midrange or going to the basket, he has all of that in the arsenal. You don't see that anymore. Now, if you go through a series of moves, and get some space and take a midrange jumper that you know you can make, it's a bad shot because it was not a three. That's just how the game is now. That's what all the analytics and numbers say. But I hope there will still be kids out there who watch Kobe and keep his style of play alive. It's not in the NBA anymore. Kobe mastered it.

That made me appreciate so much more the style of play he has, because it was the same style of play we had in the 1980s and '90s. His competitive drive and his nature of just wanting to win, it was very impressive to me. He loves to play. He has a competitive nature that you just don't see anymore. He put so much into it. He would carry that team on his back when he had to. He would play through pain. When he had his Achilles tear, I knew what that was like because I went through it, too. After he announced his retirement, when the Lakers came to Atlanta, I went to see him and I went to tell him how much I appreciated it. I told him, "I love you as a player and as a person." It was emotional, you know; it is always emotional to decide when to walk away. But I said I loved him, and I told him he might be in great shape, but starting now he is just another old guy like me.

He was a wonderful ambassador for our league. You can love him or hate him, and a lot of people did because of his competitive nature, but I will say this—he is the Last of the Mohicans. Now with him retired, our era is officially over. In 2016, at the Air Canada Centre in Toronto, Kobe Bryant completed a ritual in which he took part 18 times during his storied career: he played in the NBA's All-Star game, finishing with ten points, seven assists, and six rebounds. Bryant accepted gifts and accolades throughout the weekend and joked, "I am looking around the room and I am seeing guys that I am playing with that are tearing the league up who were like 4 during my first All-Star game. It's truly, it's—how many guys can say they played 20 years and have seen the game actually go through three, four generations?" But just as Bryant had praise for those he played with and against over the course of his All-Star career, his fellow All-Stars had praise for him.

PART 5:

QUOTES, QUIPS, AND TIDBITS

"IT WAS KIND of like the way you would do with Michael Jordan when he played. If you weren't careful, you stopped coaching, and you just started watching, because they're so incredible." *–Gregg Popovich*

Russell Westbrook

Westbrook earned five All-Star selections in his first eight seasons and teamed with Bryant in every one. He was also a teammate of Kobe's on the 2012 Olympic team.

Regular Season	Games	Wins	Losses	Win %	Field Goal %	PPG	Points (High)	RPG	APG	SPG
Bryant	22	10	12	0.455	0.414	23.5	40 (12/22/09)	4.8	5.4	1.4
Westbrook	22	12	10	0.545	0.417	22.5	37 (3/5/13)	6.1	8.2	1.5

Playoffs	Games	Wins	Losses	Win %	Field Goal %	PPG	Points (High)	RPG	APG	SPG
Bryant	11	5	6	0.455	0.418	27	42 (5/21/12)	4.5	3.9	1.5
Westbrook	11	6	5	0.545	0.479	22.8	37 (5/19/12)	5.7	5.4	1.6

ME GROWING UP in Los Angeles and being able to see Kobe, obviously he has become one of the greatest players to ever play the game. It was a true honor to be able to learn from him. To play in the Olympics with him was a great experience for me, to be able to learn different things from him, not just on the floor but off the floor, as well. When you watch his demeanor and his competitive nature, that set him apart. The mindset of having that killer instinct—I think a lot of players take that for granted, especially coming from him and him being able to have that killer instinct. That is what made him a better player, the player he is today, and it is going to be strange not to see him on the floor.

John Wall

Bryant's final All-Star game was Wall's third straight. But Wall has little trouble remembering a tougher moment against Kobe: the first time he faced off against him, back in December 2010. Wall had been the No. 1 pick in the draft six months earlier.

Regular Season	Games	Wins	Losses	Win %	Field Goal %	PPG	Points (High)	RPG	APG	SPG
Bryant	6	2	4	0.33	0.398	26.7	32 (12/7/10)	3.5	4.3	1.8
Wall	6	4	2	0.66	0.457	20.5	34 (12/2/15)	4.8	13.2	1.2

I **DO REMEMBER GOING** against him. I blocked his shot, but he got the rebound back, stepped back, and made a three-pointer, and said to me, "The play goes on, young fella." That was my first time playing against him at the Staples Center.

It's an honor to be able to play with him, to take the floor against him this season. It's a historical career, one where he didn't have success early on, but it started building up. Maybe the most competitive player I have ever played against—his heart, his determination, his drive, how much work he puts in, how much he loves the game. It's tough to think that will ever be matched. The era I've seen him play basketball, what he meant to this game and the way he is going out is in a masterful way. A lot of people are going to represent and support him. For somebody to retire, then go to every city and get that respect, and have them give him tributes for his last walk-through, it means a lot to see that. It's been great to be able to see that, and witness it. He is a guy who sacrificed everything for the game of basketball.

Gregg Popovich

Popovich has coached in four All-Star games, and Bryant was a starter in all four games. He was caught on camera trying to guard Kobe in practice during Kobe's final All-Star weekend, and, predictably, Bryant came up with an easy layup. But Popovich has long expressed his admiration for Bryant.

IT **WAS KIND** of like the way you would do with Michael Jordan when he played. If you weren't careful, you stopped coaching, and you just started watching, because they're so incredible. For us it was a lot scarier because, in his prime and in some of those moments, no matter what you did defensively he still could rise up over you and get off a relatively uncontested shot with balance. That would scare you because there's really no defense for it. It was like you couldn't let him get the ball, so you had to pick your spots when you wanted to get him away from the ball or, if he did have the ball, who you were going to send to him, who you were going to allow to shoot the ball, what you were going to give up if you went after him and took it out of his hands. It was that sort of thing. But the final fear would always be, even if we did that, he still would rise up, and he's going to get that shot off. And he did that against a lot of people, including us, many times.

But watching him, he's got the same fire, the same competitiveness. He still wants to destroy his opponents. He was like that from Day One.

Kyle Lowry

Lowry earned two All-Star spots and was playing for the host Toronto Raptors in Bryant's All-Star finale. Lowry went to Villanova and grew up in Philadelphia.

Regular Season	Games	Wins	Losses	Win %	Field Goal %	PPG	Points (High)	RPG	APG	SPG
Bryant	21	14	7	0.66	0.455	27.9	53 (3/28/08)	5.3	5.8	2.2
Lowry	21	7	14	0.33	0.393	10.6	29 (11/30/14)	4	5.2	1.2

Playoffs	Games	Wins	Losses	Win %	Field Goal %	PPG	Points (High)	RPG	APG	SPG
Bryant	7	4	3	0.571	0.453	27.4	40 (5/6/09)	5	3.7	2
Lowry	7	3	4	0.429	0.35	5.7	12 (5/10/09)	2.6	3.1	0.7

IT MEANS A lot to everybody, because he is the Michael Jordan of our era. He's the most competitive player a lot of players have ever played against. The things he has done throughout his career, the things he has done to change the game, to motivate other players, has been unbelievable. He was a Laker, and I grew up in Philadelphia, but of course he is a guy we all grew up watching and respected where he is from. He's from Philly, I am from Philly, and the things he has done to put Philly on the map, it's unmatchable. I think he is a guy who has inspired a lot of other players; that's one of the important things about his career.

Carmelo Anthony

Anthony was selected to nine out of ten All-Star games from 2007-'16 and over the years became close with Bryant. Anthony, Chris Paul, and Dwyane Wade hosted a dinner for him during All-Star weekend in Toronto, during which Anthony gave Kobe a 1996 (Bryant's rookie year) vintage Barbaresco wine. Anthony called it, "a thank-you dinner."

Regular Season	Games	Wins	Losses	Win %	Field Goal %	PPG	Points (High)	RPG	APG	SPG
Bryant	29	16	13	0.552	0.44	26.7	42 (twice)	4.9	5.2	1.4
Anthony	29	13	16	0.448	0.461	23.5	35 (2/25/04)	6.3	3.3	1.2

Playoffs	Games	Wins	Losses	Win %	Field Goal %	PPG	Points (High)	RPG	APG	SPG
Bryant	10	8	2	0.80	0.489	33.8	49 (4/23/08)	5.6	6	1.1
Anthony	10	2	8	0.20	0.388	25.5	39 (5/19/09)	6.7	3	1

HE IS A legend, a Hall of Famer, I just respect everything he did for our game. I remember being with him in the

(2008 and 2012) Olympics, and it was just amazing to see him work, to see how dedicated he is to the game. He was a big brother to me starting then, and to be able to play with him and against him over the years, that is a really big thing for me. It was a great way to send him off. We're going to miss him. It gives you chills to know you competed against a guy for so long and it is finally coming to an end. For him to get that send-off the way it happened, from us as players, from the NBA as a whole, it was a great way to send him off.

Kobe Bryant—By the Numbers

Season	Tm	G	GS	MP	FG	FG%	3P	3PA	3P%	2P	2PA	2P%	FT	FTA	FT%	ORB	DRB	TRB	AST	STL	BLK	TOV	PF	PTS	PPG
1996-97	LAL	71	6	1103	176	0.417	51	136	.375	125	286	0.437	136	166	0.819	47	85	132	91	49	23	112	102	539	17.6
1997-98	LAL	79	1	2056	391	0.428	75	220	.341	316	693	0.456	363	457	0.794	79	163	242	199	74	40	157	180	1220	21.4
1998-99	LAL	50	50	1896	362	0.465	27	101	.267	335	678	0.494	245	292	0.839	53	211	264	190	72	50	157	153	996	18.9
1999-00	LAL	66	62	2524	554	0.468	46	144	.319	508	1039	0.489	331	403	0.821	108	308	416	323	106	62	182	220	1485	21.2
2000-01	LAL	68	68	2783	701	0.464	61	200	.305	640	1310	0.489	475	557	0.853	104	295	399	338	114	43	220	222	1938	25.1
2001-02	LAL	80	80	3063	749	0.469	33	132	.250	716	1465	0.489	488	589	0.829	112	329	441	438	118	35	223	228	2019	23.7
2002-03	LAL	82	82	3401	868	0.451	124	324	.383	744	1600	0.465	601	713	0.843	106	458	564	481	181	67	288	218	2461	26
2003-04	LAL	65	64	2447	516	0.438	71	217	.327	445	961	0.463	454	533	0.852	103	256	359	330	112	28	171	176	1557	22.9
2004-05	LAL	66	66	2689	573	0.433	131	387	.339	442	937	0.472	542	664	0.816	95	297	392	398	86	53	270	174	1819	24.4
2005-06	LAL	80	80	3277	978	0.45	180	518	.347	798	1655	0.482	696	819	0.85	71	354	425	360	147	30	250	233	2832	31.1
2006-07	LAL	77	77	3140	813	0.463	137	398	.344	676	1359	0.497	667	768	0.868	75	364	439	413	111	36	255	205	2430	27.9
2007-08	LAL	82	82	3192	775	0.459	150	415	.361	625	1275	0.49	623	742	0.84	94	423	517	441	151	40	257	227	2323	26.2
2008-09	LAL	82	82	2960	800	0.467	118	336	.351	682	1376	0.496	483	564	0.856	90	339	429	399	120	37	210	189	2201	26.8
2009-10	LAL	73	73	2835	716	0.456	99	301	.329	617	1268	0.487	439	541	0.811	78	313	391	365	113	20	233	187	1970	25
2010-11	LAL	82	82	2779	740	0.451	115	356	.323	625	1283	0.487	483	583	0.828	83	336	419	388	99	12	243	172	2078	26.9
2011-12	LAL	58	58	2232	574	0.43	87	287	.303	487	1049	0.464	381	451	0.845	66	247	313	264	69	18	204	105	1616	26.1
2012-13	LAL	78	78	3013	738	0.463	132	407	.324	606	1188	0.51	525	626	0.839	66	367	433	469	106	25	287	173	2133	25.5
2013-14	LAL	6	6	177	31	0.425	3	16	.188	28	57	0.491	18	21	0.857	2	24	26	38	7	1	34	9	83	16.9
2014-15	LAL	35	35	1207	266	0.373	54	184	.293	212	529	0.401	196	241	0.813	26	173	199	197	47	7	128	65	782	23.3
2015-16	LAL	66	66	1863	398	0.358	133	467	.285	265	646	0.41	232	281	0.826	41	206	247	184	62	13	129	115	1161	22.4
Career		1346	1198	48637	11719	0.447	1837	5546	0.329	9892	20654	0.479	8378	10011	0.837	1499	5548	7047	6306	1944	640	4010	3353	33643	24.9